TRUE CRIME CASE HISTORIES

VOLUME 15

JASON NEAL

JASON NEAL BOOKS

Great effort and research have gone into the compilation of this material. It is the author's intention to represent the information within as accurately as possible. However, the author and publisher do not guarantee the accuracy of the text, graphics, and information presented. Any errors, omissions, or misinterpretations of this publication are not the responsibility of the author, copyright holder, or publisher. Although based on fact, some character names may have been changed, and/or scenes and dialogue may have been fictionalized. This publication is produced solely for informational and entertainment purposes and is not intended to hurt or defame anyone involved.

Cover images of:

Chandler Halderson: (top-left)

Sabrina Kouider: (top-right)

Don Steenkamp: (bottom-left)

Colin Pitchfork: (bottom-right)

More books by Jason Neal

Looking for more?? I am constantly adding new volumes of True Crime Case Histories. The series **can be read in any order**, and all books are available in paperback, hardcover, and audiobook.

Check out the complete series at:

https://amazon.com/author/jason-neal

All Jason Neal books are also available in **AudioBook format at Audible.com.** Enjoy a **Free Audiobook** when you signup for a 30-Day trial using this link:

https://geni.us/AudibleTrueCrime

FREE BONUS EBOOK FOR MY READERS

As my way of saying "Thank you" for downloading, I'm giving away a FREE True Crime e-book I think you'll enjoy.

https://TrueCrimeCaseHistories.com

Just visit the link above to let me know where to send your free book!

CONTENTS

INTRODUCTION

Before each book in my True Crime Case Histories series, I begin with a brief word of caution: These stories are not for the faint-hearted. Unlike true crime television shows or news reports, my books present every grim detail, regardless of how unsettling it may be. This approach isn't meant to shock but to offer insight into the criminal mind. While we may never fully comprehend their motivations, the sheer depth of their depravity will keep you turning pages.

Each narrative demands extensive research, drawing from court documents, archived news, police files, autopsies, and eyewitness reports. While I may occasionally alter names or reconstruct dialogue, these are real crimes that happened to actual people, reflecting the harsh realities of the world we live in. My commitment is to provide you with a comprehensive view of these cases.

If graphic details disturb you, this book might not be for you. But if you're ready for an unvarnished look at true crime, let's proceed.

Over the past six years, I've written more than 185 true crime stories, and I typically don't give my opinion on cases —just report the facts. However, I wanted to highlight something that's always struck me as odd about sentencing and parole and how it varies in different parts of the world.

Here in the United States, we're big on heavy punishments. As of 2023, there are more than 1.2 million people in U.S. prisons. 203,000 of those are serving a life sentence, and 55,000 are serving life without parole. That's 4.47 percent of all inmates who will never be released.

However, the numbers are drastically lower in other countries. The United Kingdom, Canada, and Australia rarely sentence an offender to life without parole.

Percentage of inmates serving life without parole.

The reason I mention these statistics is that two of the stories in this volume take place outside the U.S., and the killers become eligible for parole this year.

In one story, a man from the U.K. with a long history of sexual offenses who raped and strangled two fifteen-year-old girls is up for parole this July. He'll be sixty-four years old—still a potentially long life ahead of him.

In another story, a fifteen-year-old who raped his sister and killed his entire family to cover up the crime will be eligible for parole this year at the age of forty. If paroled, he could likely spend more of his life free than he did behind bars.

Those who have read the previous volumes of True Crime Case Histories know that I've covered similar stories throughout the years where the killer was eventually paroled and released. Some go on to kill again.

Of course, each case has its unique details, but I believe that if someone intentionally and premeditatedly takes a life, they should be imprisoned for life. With people living longer nowadays, releasing a triple murderer by the age of forty seems like a horrible injustice.

Volume 15 of True Crime Case Histories presents twelve cases spanning the past five decades. In today's true crime-saturated media landscape, finding lesser-known stories is challenging. That's where you, my readers, become invaluable. Many cases in this volume were suggested by readers like yourself, and for that, I'm deeply grateful. If you come across an obscure case worthy of investigation, please email me with any details you can remember, and I'll do my best to research it.

Lastly, please join my mailing list for discounts, updates, and a free e-book. You can sign up for that at:

TrueCrimeCaseHistories.com

Additional photos, videos, and documents pertaining to the cases in this volume can be found on the accompanying web page at:

TrueCrimeCaseHistories.com/vol15

Thanks again for reading, and I sincerely hope you gain some insight from this volume of True Crime Case Histories.

- Jason Neal

CHAPTER 1
THE SACRIFICIAL SHACK

South Padre Island—located at the southernmost tip of Texas, near where the Rio Grande river meets the Gulf of Mexico—transformed into a bustling tourist destination after Hurricane Beulah's devastation in 1967. Rebuilt with an array of popular resorts and condominiums, the island now features scenic, sandy beaches that attract visitors year-round.

Each March, South Padre Island's population swells from 1,000 to over 250,000 as students from across the country descend on the beach town for spring break, eager to enjoy the sun and fun.

In 1989, Mark Kilroy and his friends, who had been eagerly planning their spring break trip for months, were set to return to South Padre Island for the third consecutive year. Once close teammates in high school baseball and basketball, the four friends were now attending different colleges across Texas.

Mark Kilroy grew up in Santa Fe, Texas, a suburb of Houston, where he was a standout both academically and athletically from an early age. His early involvement in the Boy Scouts paved the way for a high school career filled with extracurricular activities. He excelled in sports like baseball, golf, and basketball while also serving on the student council and maintaining excellent grades. Although he received a scholarship offer for basketball, Mark was determined to pursue medicine. By the age of twenty-one, he was a junior pre-med student at the University of Texas at Austin, focused on becoming a general practice doctor.

On Friday, March 10, Mark Kilroy drove to Texas A&M University in College Station to pick up his childhood friend, Bradley Moore, a sophomore studying electrical engineering. The pair then traveled to their hometown of Santa Fe, Texas, where they picked up two more friends, Bill Huddleston and Brent Martin. With their group assembled, the four young men embarked on a six-hour journey to South Padre Island, arriving just before midnight.

The next morning, the group checked into the Sheraton Resort on Gulf Boulevard and promptly headed for the beach. It was the start of the five-week spring break season, and the crowds were still sparse. However, as the weekend approached, thousands of students from across the country were expected to flood into the town, significantly boosting its energy and activity.

Throughout the town, beer companies sponsored various free events, such as concerts, movies, and parties, drawing in the crowds. The group's favorite was the nightly Miss Tanline contest held on the beach behind their hotel.

On their second day, after breakfast, the four friends lounged by the pool, soaking up the sun before attending the Miss

Tanline contest. After lunch, they took a brief nap and then planned an excursion to Matamoros, Mexico. Just an hour's drive inland, right across the border from Brownsville, Texas, Matamoros was a popular destination for spring breakers, attracted by cheaper alcohol prices and a lower legal drinking age of eighteen.

That evening, the group left their hotel and headed for the border, stopping en route at a Sonic Drive-In for burgers. There, they met a group of girls from the University of Kansas who were also planning to visit Matamoros. After finishing their meal, they all drove to Brownsville, parked their cars, and crossed the Rio Grande into Mexico on foot using the Gateway International Bridge.

The Gateway International Bridge leads directly onto Avenida Álvaro Obregón in Mexico, a street bustling with nightclubs catering to the crowds of students visiting during spring break. That night, more than fifteen thousand revelers packed the area. Opting for the nightclub with the shortest queue, the group entered Sergeant Pepper's, where they enjoyed drinks and socialized until 2:30 in the morning. Afterward, they crossed back into Texas and returned to their hotel.

The following afternoon mirrored the previous day's activities, with the group once again enjoying the Miss Tanline competition and relaxing by the pool. In the early evening, they met up with one of Mark's fraternity brothers from college. Just after 10:30 p.m., the group made another trip to Matamoros for a night of drinking and socializing. Bill Huddleston later described the vibrant scene of thousands of students partying on the Mexican streets as "an amusement park without the rides—one big thrill."

The four friends spent the evening bar-hopping in Matamoros, starting at Los Sombrero before moving on to the London Pub, which had rebranded itself as the Hard Rock Cafe for spring break. The atmosphere was far rowdier than the previous bars they'd visited, with louder music and tourists energetically throwing beer from the balcony onto the dancing crowd below.

As the night progressed at the Hard Rock Cafe, the group ordered beers, and Mark Kilroy struck up a conversation with a girl at the bar. Amid the festive chaos, his friends lost track of him while mingling in the crowd. By 2:00 a.m., with the crowds beginning to disperse, they decided it was time to head back to the hotel, realizing Mark was no longer with them.

When Bill, Brent, and Bradley exited the nightclub, they found Mark outside on the sidewalk, deep in conversation with a girl. It turned out she was one of the Miss Tanline contestants Mark had spoken with at the hotel two days earlier.

As the four friends began their trek toward the Texas bridge, they joined thousands of other students with the same plan, navigating through the dense, intoxicated crowd. Bradley and Brent were slightly ahead, while Bill and Mark lagged a few yards behind. Mark paused at Garcia's, another bustling bar on their route, to say goodbye to a girl he had met earlier that evening. Unaware that Bill and Mark had stopped, Bradley and Brent continued toward the bridge. Meanwhile, Bill took a moment to find an alley to urinate. When he returned just a few minutes later, he discovered that Mark was no longer where he had left him.

Bill called out for Mark, but amidst the sea of students, there was no response. Assuming Mark had moved ahead to cross the bridge, Bill hurried to catch up. However, when he reached the Texas side of the river, only Bradley and Brent were there. Mark was nowhere to be found.

Bill, Bradley, and Brent re-crossed the bridge to Matamoros, searching desperately for their friend. They traversed the street and checked each bar, which had far fewer patrons by then, but there was still no sign of Mark. By 4:30 a.m., with the streets nearly empty, they returned across the bridge, hoping Mark might be waiting by their car. When they didn't find him there, they assumed he might have caught a ride back to the hotel. However, upon their return to South Padre Island, Mark was not at the hotel either. He had simply vanished.

Believing that Mark might have been thrown in jail, Bill, Brent, and Bradley drove back to Matamoros the next morning. They headed straight to the local police to inquire about their friend. However, their search yielded no results; there was no record of Mark Kilroy in police custody.

Mexican officials displayed little concern about Mark's disappearance, treating it as a routine incident. It was not uncommon for students to go missing in Matamoros during spring break, often reappearing days later after joining other party-goers. In fact, sixty missing person reports had been filed in the first three months of that year, reinforcing the officials' lackadaisical attitude toward such cases.

Mexican police assured them that Mark had likely met a girl and spent the night with her. However, Brent, Bill, and Bradley knew this wasn't right. Mark was exceptionally responsible, and such behavior was out of character for him. They were convinced something terrible had happened.

The three friends went to the American consulate in Mexico and then reported Mark's disappearance to the police in Brownsville. That evening, they checked the hotel once more, but Mark still hadn't shown up. Just after 11:00 p.m., they made the difficult call to Mark's parents, James and Helen Kilroy, informing them that their oldest son had vanished in Mexico.

Concerned about the challenges of dealing with law enforcement on both sides of the border, Mark's father reached out to his brother, Ken Kilroy, who worked for the U.S. Customs Service in Los Angeles. Leveraging his connections, Ken established a task force in Brownsville to oversee the case despite American police having no jurisdiction in Mexico.

Initially, Mexican authorities, concerned about the impact on lucrative spring break tourism, tried to suggest that Mark had disappeared in Brownsville rather than in Mexico. However, the Mexican federal police eventually agreed to cooperate with U.S. investigators. A commander assigned Mexican agents to join U.S. officials in Matamoros. Together, they interviewed informants and potential witnesses and followed up on leads from their respective sources, working diligently to uncover any information about Mark's whereabouts.

Both Mexican and U.S. authorities suspected foul play in Mark's disappearance, considering the possibility that he had fallen victim to drug-related violence or a robbery gone wrong. Despite these suspicions, the investigation struggled due to a lack of substantial leads, leaving them unable to draw any definitive conclusions.

While under hypnosis, Bill Huddleston recalled seeing a young Hispanic man with a noticeable scar across his face, dressed in a blue plaid shirt, talking with Mark Kilroy shortly before his disappearance. He remembered the man approaching Kilroy and asking, "Hey, don't I know you from somewhere?" However, Huddleston couldn't recall Mark's response. Despite this revelation, none of Mark's friends could pinpoint the exact time or location of his disappearance.

Based on the available information, investigators theorized that Mark Kilroy was likely abducted for robbery or ransom. However, the absence of any ransom demands led them to lean more toward the robbery theory. Tragically, they suspected Mark was already dead and that his body had been disposed of in a secluded area. U.S. Border Patrol helicopters conducted aerial searches while officers on ATVs scoured the Rio Grande River's edge, but their efforts yielded no results.

Mark's parents drove down to assist in any way possible. Together with volunteers, they distributed over 20,000 flyers across South Padre Island, Brownsville, and Matamoros. The family raised $15,000 to offer as a reward for information leading to their son's whereabouts, and they also sought help from prominent figures like Attorney General Jim Mattox, Texas Governor William Clements, and U.S. Senator Lloyd Bentsen to bolster the investigation.

On March 26, the case gained national attention when America's Most Wanted aired a segment about Mark's disappearance. The show generated numerous tips from phone calls and letters, but unfortunately, none proved useful in advancing the investigation.

Helen Kilroy was shocked to receive a call from a man claiming he had abducted Mark and was holding him at a drug house in Houston. The caller demanded $10,000 for Mark's release and instructed Helen to deliver the money to a cemetery, threatening to mail one of Mark's fingers if she didn't comply. However, police soon discovered that the call had been made by two men already in custody on extortion charges at the Galveston County Jail.

After three weeks of searching for their son, the Kilroy family realized there was nothing more they could do on the ground and returned to Santa Fe. Back home, the community rallied in support, organizing garage sales and car washes to raise funds for the family's continued search efforts. In a heart-wrenching move, James and Helen Kilroy traveled to the University of Texas at Austin to withdraw their son from school.

The first break in the case came from an unrelated incident three weeks after Mark went missing. In early April, the U.S. Customs Service informed Mexican federales about a recent surge in drugs crossing the border into Mexico. This prompted a massive anti-drug operation involving over 1,000 agents, twelve helicopters, and thirty airplanes patrolling the border near Matamoros.

The federales had set up a drug interdiction checkpoint along Mexican Federal Highway 2, just outside of Matamoros, inspecting each car crossing the U.S.-Mexico border. On April 1, however, a man in a pickup truck ignored the armed officers and sped through the roadblock, entering Mexico without stopping.

One of the officers recognized the driver as Serafín Hernández García, a brazen twenty-year-old from a family with deep roots in the drug trade.

Instead of using their sirens to pull the truck over, two undercover officers in an unmarked police car discreetly followed it for twenty miles west of Matamoros until it pulled into the Santa Elena ranch. Suspecting the ranch was involved in drug operations, they refrained from approaching. Instead, they parked on a side road and observed the ranch from a distance, gathering information.

After about thirty minutes, the driver left the ranch and headed back to the city. Seizing the opportunity, the officers decided to act and initiated a search of the ranch.

Driving down the half-mile dirt driveway, the officers arrived at a large steel warehouse next to a weathered reddish-brown wooden shack and livestock pens. In front of the warehouse, several new, high-end cars and trucks were lined up. Inspecting a nearby blue Chevy Suburban, they were surprised to find a car phone installed, a rare luxury in 1989. Inside the SUV, they discovered traces of marijuana and a stone statue that they recognized as occult paraphernalia, which immediately heightened their suspicions.

While inspecting the cars, the officers were approached by a man who introduced himself as Domingo, the ranch's caretaker. To maintain their cover, the officers pretended to be lost and asked for directions back to Matamoros. Noticing Domingo's unease, they decided to leave the ranch, planning to return later with a more strategic approach.

Upon learning about the new, expensive cars at the Santa Elena ranch, police realized the Hernandez drug operation was far more lucrative than anticipated and placed the ranch under surveillance for several days. Investigators also identified the statue in the SUV as Elegua, a deity of the roads in Palo Mayombe, an Afro-Cuban religion. Elegua was believed to protect followers during their travels or while smuggling drugs.

Eight days later, a team of Mexican police returned to Santa Elena, seizing 243 pounds of marijuana, a dozen guns (including three submachine guns), and eleven luxury cars, some equipped with car phones. Serafín Hernández García, his uncle Elio Hernández Rivera, David Serna Valdez, and Sergio Martínez Salinas were arrested on drug trafficking charges.

However, the men were calm and relaxed during questioning and refused to answer.

While police searched the property, the caretaker, Domingo Reyes Bustamante, had shown up for work unaware that his employers had been arrested. Upon questioning, Domingo freely admitted that Serafín and Elio had been running a drug smuggling operation.

As officers questioned Domingo, they showed him a photo of Mark Kilroy and asked if he had ever seen him. Domingo nodded and said, "Yeah, I seen him," and motioned toward the small run-down shack.

Domingo recounted a tale of horror. He told investigators that Mark Kilroy had arrived at the ranch in the back of the blue Chevy Suburban. He had been abducted, bound, gagged, and blindfolded. Mark was left in the SUV overnight, and in the morning, Domingo gave him eggs, bread, and water. Hours later, his bosses took Mark away, but Domingo was unaware of what happened to him after that.

When investigators learned that Mark Kilroy had been to the ranch, they intensified their interrogation of the four arrested men. Serafín, displaying a cocky demeanor, eventually admitted that Mark Kilroy and several other men had died at the ranch.

Serafin told investigators that the killings had been ordered by Adolfo Constanzo, a Cuban-American who was the leader of a cult that they all belonged to. Constanzo practiced a ritual form of human sacrifice. He and his followers believed the sacrifice of human victims provided strength, riches, and immunity from law enforcement. Serafin and others in the Hernandez drug family referred to Constanzo as their Godfather or "El Padrino."

Serafin spoke to investigators with a disturbing sense of detachment, as if he believed that their abhorrent actions were justified by their religious beliefs.

The next day, Mexican officials and American investigators accompanied Serafín back to Santa Elena. He showed no signs of remorse and appeared utterly unaffected by the consequences he faced.

When American investigators approached the small shack, they instantly smelled the putrid smell of decomposition. However, Mexican investigators hesitated to enter the shack due to the prevalent beliefs in witchcraft, the occult, and superstition in Mexican culture.

Investigators ushered Serafin into the shack, where the flickering light of two lit candles revealed recent activity. Inside, four pots contained a macabre assortment: a dead rooster, a goat's head, coins, sticks, a turtle, and another Elegua statue. The floor was strewn with cigar butts, chili peppers, and various bottles, creating an unsettling atmosphere.

Dark stains of dried blood peppered the walls, and a wire hook hung from the rafters above. Serafin told investigators that the hook was used to hold victims' wrists while their blood was drained from them into a large iron cauldron in the center of the room called an nganga. In the Palo Mayombe religion, the nganga is a sacred cauldron that houses the spirit of the dead. This spirit, believed to reside within the nganga, acts as a spiritual guide and a powerful presence during all rituals and ceremonies performed with the vessel.

The nganga was filled with a sacrificial stew: a sickening mix of chicken feet, sticks, a turtle, a dead black cat, human hair, a goat's head, a horseshoe, pieces of human brain, and a broth made of blood. Serafin told investigators that Mark Kilroy's brains were still in the cauldron.

Without regard for the active crime scene, Mexican authorities, who were much more superstitious than the American investigators, ordered Serafin to drag the cauldron out of the shack. They then shot their guns in the air and did their best to destroy the inside of the shack.

When Serafin was asked what happened to Mark Kilroy's remains, he pointed toward the livestock pens. In the corner of the pen, a long piece of heavy wire stuck three feet out of the ground. Serafin explained the wire was attached to Mark's spinal column. Once the body had decomposed, they had planned to pull up the wire with his vertebrae attached so they could thread it into a necklace.

Disgusted, Mexican investigators threw shovels at Serafin and the three other men and, at gunpoint, ordered him to dig. As he dug, Serafin commented, "I don't know why they're making such a big deal of this one here. There's another guy there. And another guy over there." Serafin pointed to other spots in the pen.

Altogether, the four men unearthed fifteen mutilated bodies in various stages of decomposition from the ground near the shack. All were men who had been murdered over the past nine months. Some had been skinned alive, while others were severely burned. Most of the bodies found were later identified as members of rival drug gangs, but three men remained unidentified.

Mark Kilroy's legs had been severed at the knees, and his skull had a gaping hole where his brain had been removed. When asked if cutting off the legs was part of the ritual, Serafin told investigators matter-of-factly that it wasn't. It simply made him easier to bury.

Serafín Hernández García went into great detail during questioning and explained how they had abducted Mark Kilroy. He said that Constanzo had ordered his men to find a white, Anglo man to sacrifice.

On the evening of March 14, Serafín and several other men from their cult went to the busy streets of Matamoros, searching through the thousands of spring break students for a victim. They spotted Mark Kilroy standing on the street. One of the men struck up a conversation with him, luring him closer to their truck. As Mark approached, they grabbed him from behind and shoved him into the vehicle.

As they sped away from Avenida Álvaro Obregón, Mark seized his first opportunity to leap from the truck and run. However, a blue Chevy Suburban with more cult members quickly caught up to him. They cornered him at gunpoint, handcuffed him, and forced him into the back of the SUV.

Mark Kilroy was driven twenty miles out of town to the Santa Elena ranch, where he was left in the back of the SUV for the next twelve hours.

When Adolfo Constanzo arrived the next day, Mark's mouth was duct-taped shut. With his arms still secured behind his back, they pulled him from the SUV and walked him to the sacrificial shack.

For hours throughout the night of March 15, Mark Kilroy was brutally tortured and sodomized by Constanzo. The following morning, Constanzo dragged Mark out of the shack into a field, where he used a large machete to chop the back of his neck and head.

Constanzo then removed his brain, put it in the nganga, and boiled it in a ceremonial stew. Cult members then severed his legs, inserted the wire into his spinal column, and buried him near the other fourteen bodies.

On April 12, the Mexican Federal Judicial Police in Matamoros held a press conference to address the hundreds of journalists who had flocked to the city to cover the horrific story. The media had dubbed the cult "the Narcosatanists."

They allowed the press to speak directly to the four suspects. During the conference, the men displayed no signs of remorse, claiming their actions brought them power and protection. Elio explained that he was an ordained executioner under Constanzo, but that Constanzo had personally killed Mark Kilroy. Serafín proudly showed the cameras the arrow-shaped scars covering his arms, chest, back, and shoulders. These scars, made with a searing-hot knife, signified his membership in the cult and granted him the authority to perform human sacrifices.

Two weeks after the bodies were discovered at Santa Elena, Mexican federal police, driven by fear and superstition, returned to the ranch at dawn to burn the shack to the ground. They brought in a curandero, a traditional healer, to purify the shack before its destruction. The curandero entered the shack, uttered prayers, scattered salt on the floor, and concluded with the sign of the cross.

The Mexican police then doused the shack with gasoline and set it ablaze, disregarding the importance of preserving the crime scene before the prosecution of the suspects.

While the Mexican government provided no official rationale for their actions, a source connected to the investigation suggested that the police's motives were rooted in supernatural beliefs.

They believed that burning down the shack, which held significance for Constanzo, would deeply affect him. The morning after the arson was broadcast on national television, Constanzo, who was still at large, reportedly flew into a rage. An international manhunt began to bring Constanzo and his followers to justice.

Adolfo Constanzo was born in Miami in 1962 to a teenage Cuban immigrant named Delia González. Although he was baptized Catholic and served as an altar boy, Adolfo's spiritual path took a dark turn when his mother introduced him to the mysteries of Vodou during their trips to Haiti.

As a teenager in Miami, Constanzo became fascinated by the occult. He apprenticed himself to a local sorcerer and immersed himself in the practice of Palo Mayombe, an African religion involving animal sacrifice. Upon moving to Mexico City as an adult, Constanzo leveraged his dark arts for profit, offering ritual sacrifices and casting spells for good luck. His clientele, a dangerous mix of wealthy drug dealers and corrupt policemen, welcomed him into the shadowy world of Mexico's powerful drug cartels.

Constanzo's ambition and cruelty grew hand in hand. He demanded a full partnership in a cartel, and when the family dared to refuse him, seven of their members vanished only to reappear later as mutilated corpses. By the late 1980s, Constanzo's cult had claimed over twenty lives in grisly ritual murders, their bodies desecrated for arcane sacrifices.

At his side stood twenty-four-year-old Sara Aldrete, a promising college student in Brownsville who lived just across the border in Matamoros. By day, she was a model student and respected member of the school community. By night, she was a high-ranking member of Adolfo Constanzo's cult, deeply involved in drug smuggling and ritual murders.

Standing at an impressive 6'1" and excelling in her physical education studies, Sara Aldrete stood out from her peers. She dreamed of becoming a teacher and was preparing to transfer to a university to pursue her certification. At Texas Southmost College, she was known as a bright, hardworking, and friendly student. She majored in physical education, played on the soccer team, excelled as an honor student, and served as a cheerleader and president of the soccer booster club. In 1988, she was named "Outstanding Physical Education Student" and was listed in the school's "Who's Who." She also worked part-time in the athletics department and was well-liked by classmates and professors alike.

However, unbeknownst to those around her, Aldrete led a completely different life in Mexico. She was introduced to Constanzo in 1987 by her boyfriend, a drug dealer, and quickly became deeply involved in his cult.

Constanzo saw something in Sara that he could manipulate and mold to his twisted desires. He nicknamed her "La Madrina," the godmother, and initiated her into his cult, which was a terrifying blend of Santería, Aztec warrior rituals, and Palo Mayombe.

As Sara fell deeper under Constanzo's spell, he elevated her to second-in-command of his cult. While he focused on shipping marijuana across the border into the United States, Sara supervised his followers. She had become a key figure in a nightmare world of violence and depravity, a stark contrast to the bright and ambitious student she had once been.

In Matamoros, Aldrete lived in her parents' house, where she maintained an altar dedicated to occult practices. She was believed to have actively participated in the cult's brutal rituals and murders. Some investigators even suspected that she played a role in selecting victims for the cult's human sacrifices.

Tips poured in, reporting sightings of Constanzo and Aldrete in Chicago, Brownsville, Miami, and New Mexico.

Mexican authorities raided Sara Aldrete's home in Matamoros, where they discovered an altar, various cult paraphernalia, and blood spatters on the walls.

On April 17, DEA officers in Houston arrested Serafín's father, Serafín Hernández Rivera Sr., along with two other Mexican men, Quintana Rodríguez and Ponce Torres, on charges of importing marijuana, drug possession, and conspiracy. Although they seized drugs, cash, and weapons, officers found no indication that these men had been involved in the cult killings.

Constanzo had connections to a $20 million cocaine operation in Houston, and police suspected he might be hiding in one of the many homes he had purchased there. However, despite several searches, there was no sign of him or Aldrete.

Adolfo Constanzo had been hiding in a Holiday Inn in Brownsville on the day the bodies were discovered. Upon hearing the news of the raid at the Santa Elena ranch, he fled to Mexico City, where he owned an apartment. He took several of his cult followers with him, including Sara Aldrete, Martín Quintana Rodríguez, Omar Francisco Orea Ochoa, and Álvaro De León Valdés.

Days later in Mexico City, officers raided one of Constanzo's homes. Although they didn't find any of the fugitive cult members, they discovered Aldrete's purse, leading them to suspect that Constanzo might have killed her. Inside the home, they also found piles of homosexual pornography and a hidden cult altar.

In early May, Mexican police were alerted that a man at a Mexico City supermarket was attempting to buy a large amount of groceries using U.S. one-hundred-dollar bills. Police followed the man to an apartment in the Rio Sena area. After several days of surveillance, authorities identified the man as Álvaro De León, one of the fugitive cult members. He had been trying to buy groceries for Constanzo, Aldrete, and the others.

On May 5, 1989, police blocked the city streets from cars and pedestrians and surrounded the building. Constanzo, barricaded inside, noticed the police presence from his apartment window and opened fire on the officers below. Amidst the exchange of gunfire, Constanzo began hurling gold coins and paper currency out of the windows. Inside the apartment, he set more cash ablaze on the stove, shouting that if he couldn't have it, no one could.

After a forty-five-minute shootout, Constanzo realized he was running out of ammunition and couldn't win. He ordered De León to kill him and Quintana Rodríguez. When De León hesitated, Constanzo beat him repeatedly in the face, threatening that he would be tortured in hell if he didn't comply. After saying his final goodbyes to his fellow cult members, Constanzo instructed De León to open fire. De León obeyed, using a machine gun to kill Constanzo and Quintana Rodríguez.

As the police stormed into the apartment, Sara Aldrete dashed from the doorway, her voice filled with terror as she cried out that Constanzo had gone mad and was dead. When De León and Aldrete were arrested, De León admitted to participating in Mark Kilroy's murder and several other killings at Santa Elena. However, he emphasized that Constanzo was responsible for the majority of the deaths.

Sara Aldrete, however, admitted nothing. She claimed to have had no knowledge of Mark Kilroy's murder until she saw it on the news. She insisted she wasn't a fully-fledged cult member, only in the initial stages of initiation. When asked why she fled to Mexico with Constanzo, she claimed she had been taken against her will and was Constanzo's captive. Aldrete refuted any suggestion of love for Constanzo, stating she was merely a follower of his teachings.

Along with another raid in Mexico City that day, seven cult members were apprehended and detained on charges of homicide, criminal association, wounding an officer, and property damage. Concerned that Constanzo might have staged his own death, investigators took his fingerprints to verify his identity and ultimately confirmed that it was indeed Constanzo who had died.

The following month, Salvador Alarcón, a Federal Judicial Police chief, was indicted for drug trafficking after it was discovered that he had acted as the cult's contact within the police. Investigators also learned that two men had been killed at Santa Elena as a favor for Alarcón.

In February 1990, cult member Orea Ochoa died after being diagnosed with AIDS. On his deathbed, he revealed that he and Aldrete had both been lovers with Constanzo, though Aldrete showed no symptoms of the disease. In August 1990, Álvaro De León was sentenced to thirty years in prison for the murders of Constanzo and Martín Quintana Rodríguez.

In May 1994, Elio and Serafín were each sentenced to sixty-seven years in prison. Their sentences included thirty-one years for multiple homicides, twelve years for possession of narcotics, five years for involvement in organized crime, two years for impersonating police officers, two years for illegal body desecration, and ten years for possessing weapons exclusive to the Mexican Armed Forces.

Sara Aldrete received a sixty-two-year prison sentence for similar charges, excluding the weapons charge, resulting in a five-year reduction compared to Elio and Serafín's sentences.

In 2003, Sara Aldrete spoke to the media and professed her innocence, claiming that police had tortured her into confessing. She alleged that they had stripped her naked, blindfolded her, hung her by her feet, beaten her upside down, and torn out her toenails. Serafín and Elio, interviewed by the press in 2014, recounted similar stories of torture by police.

American authorities have stated that if Sara Aldrete is ever released from prison in Mexico, she will immediately face charges in the U.S. for the murder of Mark Kilroy.

In the months following Mark's death, James and Helen Kilroy established the Mark Kilroy Foundation, a non-profit dedicated to drug education and prevention. The foundation's mission focused on advocating the "Just Say No" campaign and raising awareness about the dangers of drug abuse.

CHAPTER 2
WEB OF LIES

Cathryn Mellender had dated Chandler Halderson since she was eighteen, and despite their ups and downs during their two-year relationship, she thought the world of him. She even saved his contact in her phone as "Hubby," but they were nowhere close to marriage. She was still a teenager, and he was just twenty. Perhaps it was just Cathryn's passing dream.

At twenty-three, Chandler Halderson was a young man with a plan. He was ready to leave behind the small Wisconsin town where they had both grown up. Raised in Windsor, a small suburb north of Madison, Chandler had set his sights on the sunny shores of Florida, planning his move for the summer of 2021.

Chandler grew up as a typical all-American kid. He was popular, fit, and good-looking. He played soccer, excelled as a swimmer on the high school team, and earned the rank of Eagle Scout in the Boy Scouts.

Chandler had a keen interest in computers. After high school, he enrolled in Madison Area Technical College to pursue a degree in Information Technology. Just months into his studies, he secured a part-time position as a teaching assistant at the school. He had ambitious dreams of landing a high-paying job at a major tech firm.

However, early in their relationship, Chandler was unfaithful to Cathryn. He bragged to friends about hooking up with other women, and in their small town, word eventually got back to Cathryn. Heartbroken, she confronted him, and Chandler apologized profusely, promising to never stray again. To prove his commitment, he shared his location on Snapchat so she could always know where he was. Cathryn forgave him, and their relationship grew stronger.

In late 2020, as the COVID-19 pandemic led to remote work, Chandler landed an internship as an IT administrator for American Family Insurance. While still living with his parents, Chandler locked himself in his bedroom each morning and worked from home.

Chandler's parents, Bart and Krista Halderson, couldn't have been prouder of their son and his ambition to do something with his life. He consistently earned good grades and now seemed to be working steadily toward a successful career in IT. Fifty-year-old Bart Halderson worked at an accounting firm in Madison, and fifty-three-year-old Krista had been a stay-at-home mother while Chandler and his older brother Mitchell were growing up, but in recent years she had taken a job as a receptionist at an auto dealership.

Mitchell was just eighteen months older than Chandler and had taken a job with a local tech firm, but he still lived near the parents' home.

It seemed that life was going well for Chandler, and it was about to get even better. In the spring of 2021, he announced that he had just landed his dream job. Starting in the summer, he would be moving to Florida to start his new position at SpaceX, the aerospace company founded by billionaire Elon Musk. He would soon be working for the revolutionary company that designs, manufactures, and launches spacecraft and rockets.

Despite having worked at American Family Insurance for several months, Chandler had yet to receive a paycheck. He continued to borrow money from his parents, showing his father a lengthy email exchange with a human resources manager who assured him that his paycheck was on its way.

To complicate matters, Chandler's brother, Mitchell, had been diagnosed with type 1 diabetes, and in early June 2021, Chandler fell down a flight of stairs, receiving a concussion and a neck brace. But Chandler's troubles were far from over.

On July 2, the Friday before the July Fourth weekend, Krista Halderson's coworkers were concerned when she hadn't shown up for work. It wasn't like her to take a day off without letting her supervisor know first. They texted and called her phone but received no response.

Krista's coworker and close friend, Dan Kroninger, was concerned about her and decided to drive to the Halderson home and check on her. When he arrived and got no answer after knocking on the door, Dan looked in the windows and noticed nothing unusual besides a coffee table tipped on its side. He then looked in the garage window and noticed both Krista and Bart's vehicles were inside. Puzzled, Dan walked around to the back of the house as Chandler walked out of the back door wearing a towel and a bandage around one of his toes.

Chandler explained that he had been in the shower when Dan knocked at the front door. He said he had cut his toe on broken glass near the fireplace. When Dan asked about Krista, Chandler said his parents had gone to the family cabin in northern Wisconsin early that morning with another couple. He mentioned that the cabin was in White Lake, about three hours away, and he couldn't reach her by phone due to poor reception in that area.

Dan went back to work and asked Chandler to have his mother call him if he spoke to her, but the call never came.

That Sunday, which was the Fourth of July, Dan called Chandler to check if he had heard from his parents and invited him over to watch the fireworks. Chandler told Dan that he had received a text from his mother earlier that morning, informing him that they would be returning on Monday.

The text read,

> Made it safely, can't get anything through. And yes, it's packed. Going to White Lake today for the parade and will be home Monday night / Tuesday early. Love you lots!!

Monday, however, came and went with no word from Bart or Krista Halderson.

By Wednesday, July 7, Dan had become increasingly concerned and told Chandler it was time for him to report his parents missing. That morning, Chandler walked into the Dane County Sheriff's office to report that he hadn't seen his parents since July 1.

Chandler Halderson told detectives that his parents had gone to their cabin in White Lake, Wisconsin, with another couple, but he had no idea who they were. He said he had only received one text from his mother because the cellular service at the cabin was notoriously bad.

Television crews flocked to the Halderson home, eager to interview Chandler. Reluctant to appear on camera, Chandler told reporters that he hadn't seen his parents leave but knew they had left town with another couple, whom he did not know.

The search for Bart and Krista Halderson began immediately. While Mitchell was searching near the cabin, Chandler went door-to-door in the neighborhood to ask if anyone had security camera footage that might show which car his parents left in that day.

What Chandler didn't realize was that police had already gathered the footage from his neighbor's home security cameras. Although the cameras had a clear view of the Halderson home, none of the footage showed Bart and Krista leaving that morning.

On the morning of July 8, Mitchell Halderson and Krista's sister met with Langlade County Sheriff's deputies at the cabin near White Lake, but it was empty. It was apparent no one had been there in quite a while. Also, despite what Chandler had claimed, cellular service at the cabin was just fine.

Detectives back in Dane County became increasingly suspicious of Chandler's story when they discovered that the Haldersons had never visited the cabin. Additionally, they learned there was no parade in White Lake on the Fourth of July, contrary to what Chandler had claimed his mother had texted him.

Detectives suspected Chandler was involved in his parents' disappearance, though the extent of his involvement was unclear. That evening, they arrested Chandler Halderson for providing false information about a missing person.

Police interviewed Chandler's girlfriend, Cathryn Mellender, who reported that she had spent the weekend with Chandler at her family's farm. They swam in the pool and watched the fireworks on Sunday.

During the interview, Cathryn told detectives that she had spent most of the weekend with Chandler, which seemed normal. However, she recalled one crucial detail. On Saturday morning, Chandler had told her he would be at home doing chores all morning and asked her to bring some cleaning supplies to his house.

However, when she checked his location on Snapchat later that day, she found that he was nowhere near his home. The app showed him thirty-five miles away in a forested area in Prairie du Sac, Wisconsin, near the banks of the Wisconsin River. Suspicious of what her boyfriend was doing so far away from home, she took a screenshot of his location and showed it to detectives.

Investigators then spoke to Cathryn's parents to verify that Chandler had been at the farm. They said that Chandler had mentioned that he might not be able to accept the job offer from SpaceX in Florida because of his neck injury. But then Cathryn's mother had noticed something odd.

Despite the severity of the injury, Chandler had taken the brace off to swim and play in the pool. He seemed just fine.

Cathryn's parents informed investigators that Chandler had been in their pool for a few hours. Afterward, they noticed his SUV with the back hatch up parked in a field bordering a wooded area. Within minutes, they watched Chandler walk out of the woods. Days later, they noticed the ominous sign of vultures circling in the area.

On July 10, investigators went to the location where Chandler had been seen exiting the woods. Just a short distance into the wooded area, they made a gruesome discovery: a dismembered male torso covered with branches. It was the body of Bart Halderson—minus his arms, legs, and head.

Bullet wounds revealed he had been shot twice with a rifle before he was dismembered. One shot had pierced his abdomen, while another had lodged in his spinal column. Not far from the torso, they found a tarp covered in both Bart's and Krista's blood.

Investigators found an abandoned oil drum near where Cathryn's parents had seen Chandler's car. Inside the drum were broken saw blades, bolt cutters, and scissors covered in blood.

Investigators searching the Halderson home found a shell casing consistent with the bullet lodged in Bart's spine. They would later find an SKS rifle hidden in the walls of the garage.

Four days later, sniffer dogs searched the wooded area where Cathryn's Snapchat showed Chandler had been on Saturday, July 3. Deep among the brush and trees, they found the legs of his mother, Krista Halderson.

On July 15, Chandler Halderson was officially charged with the first-degree intentional homicide of his father and mutilation of a corpse.

Over the next month, authorities searched local landfills and forested areas and drained nearby ponds, looking for the remaining pieces of Bart and Krista Halderson.

Investigators found that in the days following the murders, Chandler had conducted several disturbing web searches on his computer, including terms like "Woman Wisconsin River," "Dismembered body found," and "Woman's body found Wisconsin." He had also read multiple articles about Peter Kupaza, a man in Wisconsin who had dismembered his wife and placed her body parts in bags that were later discovered in the Wisconsin River.

Krista Halderson's cell phone, which Chandler claimed his mother had used to send her last text message, was discovered wrapped in aluminum foil and concealed inside a shoe found at the Halderson home.

Investigators found more than 200 bone fragments in the fireplace of the home, which contained the DNA of Chandler's parents. Additionally, they discovered blood evidence and indications of a cleanup in the basement.

On August 25, Chandler Halderson was officially charged with the murder of his mother. Following the charges, investigators uncovered that Chandler's life had been a continuous series of lies and deception.

Investigators were left grappling with one lingering question: Why would a young man, seemingly with a promising future, murder his parents? As they delved deeper into Chandler's personal life, they discovered that his entire existence was built on lies.

Chandler Halderson had fabricated much of his life; he was not a student at Madison Area Technical College or any other school. He had never been a teaching assistant, nor had he ever interned at American Family Insurance. When he spent hours locked in his bedroom claiming to be working, he was actually playing video games.

Chandler Halderson's life was a complete fabrication, including his supposed dream job at SpaceX in Florida. He'd kept his web of lies hidden from everyone—his friends, his brother Mitchell, and his girlfriend Cathryn, who believed she would be moving to Florida with him. Chandler had even gone as far as to claim he had purchased a car and rented an apartment there. Even his reported neck injury was a lie, concocted as an excuse for why the SpaceX job fell through.

Chandler Halderson went to great lengths to maintain his lies, crafting fake emails to explain why he hadn't received any paychecks from American Family Insurance. He also staged phone calls to his father, impersonating a college advisor from Madison Area Technical College.

The situation escalated in late June when Bart and Krista Halderson began to suspect their son was not being truthful. On June 30, Bart contacted Madison Area Technical College to request Chandler's transcript and degree verification but was shocked to discover that Chandler had never been registered there. All the emails Chandler had shown his father, purportedly from a college advisor, were fabricated; no advisor by that name existed at the college.

Just minutes after his conversation with an admissions representative from the college, Bart sent a text to Chandler informing him that he had spoken to the school and that they needed to talk. The next day, between 3:00 and 5:00 p.m., Chandler murdered his parents.

The last text Bart sent to his son read,

> I'm ready when you are.

Despite the overwhelming evidence against him, Chandler Halderson entered a plea of not guilty. The prosecution presented a case arguing that Chandler had dismembered his parents and scattered their remains across Dane County, including public lands, farms, garbage cans, rivers, and ditches.

The defense argued that the evidence against Chandler Halderson was merely coincidental and insufficient to prove that he had murdered his parents. They didn't call any witnesses, and Chandler chose not to testify. Despite their arguments, Chandler was found guilty of two counts each of first-degree intentional homicide, lying to investigators, mutilating a corpse, and hiding a corpse. On March 17, 2022, he was sentenced to life in prison without the possibility of parole.

CHAPTER 3

THE GRIEKWASTAD FARM MURDERS

Griekwastad, a small town in South Africa's Northern Cape province, lies along the picturesque Orange River. This semi-arid region is celebrated for its rugged beauty, with rocky outcrops, scrubland, and fertile riverbanks defining the landscape. In 2012, life in Griekwastad mirrored that of many rural South African communities, being centered around agriculture and enriched by a strong sense of community.

The Steenkamp family held a prominent and respected place in Griekwastad's farming community. Deon Steenkamp, a burly man with a serious demeanor, owned and managed five farms. Despite his busy schedule, he also coached local children's teams in tent-pegging, a popular equestrian sport in the area. His wife, Christelle, juggled running a successful biscuit-making business from their farm, volunteering at the local church, and working as a journalist for a local newspaper. Their children, fifteen-year-old Don and fourteen-year-old Marthella, attended boarding school but cherished their weekends at home with their parents.

On the evening of Good Friday, April 6, 2012, Griekwastad's tranquility was shattered. Don Steenkamp, drenched in blood, burst into the local police station, panic etched across his face. Breathless and trembling, the teenager struggled to find his words as he approached the front desk. The officer on duty quickly led the shaken boy into a private room, attempting to calm him and piece together the night's horrific events.

With trembling hands and a quivering voice, Don recounted a chilling tale. He told police that he had heard gunshots coming from the main house while working in the barn earlier that evening. Paralyzed with fear, he hid in the barn for about fifteen minutes until the noise subsided. Summoning his courage, Don rushed to the house, only to be confronted with a scene of unimaginable horror.

Inside, Don found the lifeless bodies of his parents, Deon and Christelle, lying in pools of blood. Nearby, his sister Marthella was critically injured, clinging to life. Don rushed to her side, cradling her as she whispered her final words of love before drawing her last breath.

Overwhelmed by the gruesome sight and the loss of his family, Don gently laid Marthella down. In a daze, he stumbled outside and got into his father's pickup truck.

As he sped away from the farm, Don recalled hearing more gunshots echoing behind him. Near the main gate, he spotted a rifle and a revolver lying in the grass. Instinctively, he stopped, collected the weapons, and placed them in the truck before driving toward town. Along the way, he briefly stopped at the farm workers' quarters, warning them of the danger and urging them to take cover.

Officers listened intently to Don's account, their years of experience telling them that the boy was in a state of profound shock. They gently pressed for more details about the intruder, but Don, still reeling from the trauma, could provide no further information. Officers reassured the boy that he was safe now and promised to do everything possible to bring the perpetrator to justice.

As the gravity of the situation sank in, the small police station erupted into a frenzy of activity. Officers were dispatched to secure the crime scene at the Steenkamp farm, while others began the arduous task of breaking the news to the family's relatives and friends. The once-peaceful community of Griekwastad found itself grappling with the unthinkable—the loss of three beloved members of their tight-knit community in a brutal and senseless act of violence.

Violent farm attacks had become a grim reality in the country's rural areas. These attacks often involved robbery, assault, and even murder, leaving farming communities in a constant state of fear and unease. While such crimes were less common in Griekwastad compared to other parts of the country, a few isolated incidents over the years left the community on edge.

As the police officers approached the farmhouse, they noticed the lights were still on inside, but an eerie silence hung over the property. The officers cautiously entered the house, weapons drawn, and began to search the premises.

Inside, they discovered a gruesome scene. In the living room, they found the body of forty-four-year-old Deon Steenkamp lying in a pool of blood. He had been shot three times—once in the right shoulder, once behind the ear, and once in the chest. In addition to the bullet wounds, Deon had also suffered blunt force injuries to his head, likely caused by the butt of a gun. The position of his body and the nature of his injuries suggested that he had attempted to confront the attacker before being shot and beaten.

A few feet away, near the kitchen, lay the bodies of Don's mother, forty-three-year-old Christelle Steenkamp, and his fourteen-year-old sister, Marthella.

Christelle had been shot three times in her shoulder, neck, and back. The location and trajectory of the bullets indicated that she had been shot from behind, possibly while trying to flee or protect her daughter.

Marthella was found lying next to her mother. She had suffered the most extensive and brutal injuries among the three victims. Marthella had been shot four times, twice in the body and twice in the head. The head wounds, in particular, were described as execution-style shots. In addition to the gunshot wounds, Marthella had also sustained severe blunt force trauma to her head, believed to be from the butt of a gun, like her father.

Police also found a large pool of Marthella's blood near a tree outside the house, close to the barn. This evidence, along with blood spatters near the back door, indicated that Marthella had been shot and beaten outside before managing to crawl back into the house, where she finally succumbed to her injuries.

Marthella's blood also covered the telephone, which lay with its receiver off the hook, indicating that she had unsuccessfully tried to call for help.

Ballistic tests later showed that the two guns that Don had recovered near the gate were the murder weapons — a .357 Magnum revolver and a .22 caliber rifle. Both belonged to the father, Deon Steenkamp.

The most disturbing revelation, however, was a forensic examination performed on Marthella. Don's younger sister had suffered a much more violent attack than her parents and was brutally raped before her death. Her wounds were described as torturous and gruesome. However, the pathologist determined the sexual assault had occurred between twelve and twenty-four hours before her murder. This timing suggested the rape and the killing were separate incidents.

The pathologist also noted that the attack had been violent enough to reopen a previous injury, suggesting that it wasn't the first time the young girl had been sexually abused.

Detectives, puzzled by this finding, withheld information about Marthella's rape initially to further investigate its connection to the murders.

Investigators analyzed the blood patterns and body positions, concluding that Christelle was the first to be shot from behind with a revolver. Marthella was shot next but managed to survive briefly, running out the back door. Deon was shot last, seemingly while running toward the attacker, who then fired a second shot and beat him over the head. The killer then went outside, found Marthella hiding beneath a tree, shot her in the face, and struck her in the head with the butt of the gun.

Amazingly, Marthella was still alive and managed to stagger back into the house, reaching for the phone before collapsing next to her mother. The killer then returned with the rifle and shot each of them one final time.

While farm attacks were common, the perpetrators typically stole valuables. In the Steenkamp's case, however, only a set of keys and a knife were missing.

If an attacker had intended to steal, there was plenty to take. The gun safe was open, with the keys still dangling from the keyhole. The safe contained several guns, and none were missing except the two murder weapons. Cell phones were left in plain sight on the countertops, along with Deon's wallet, which held nearly $500 in cash and credit cards. Televisions and computers were untouched. Several vehicles in the shed had keys in the ignition, yet none were taken.

There were no signs of forced entry, nothing was ransacked, and the four family dogs were unharmed. It was clear this wasn't a robbery. Detectives also believed the killer was familiar with the layout of the home.

Investigators brought Don Steenkamp back to the farm to recount the events of the night of the murders. Don explained that earlier in the afternoon, he, his father, and his sister had watched television together while his mother was on the computer. He then worked in the barn for about forty-five minutes before hearing gunshots coming from inside the house.

Frightened, Don hid in the barn for another ten minutes before running to the house. Upon arriving, he found his sister still alive. He held Marthella close as she was dying, and in her last moments, she grabbed his shirt and ripped it, using her final breath to tell him she loved him.

The t-shirt she had ripped, however, was not the shirt he was wearing when he came into the police station. Don led investigators to his bedroom, where he showed them the blood-soaked shirt. He explained that he had changed shirts because he was repulsed by the sight and smell of his sister's blood on the fabric.

Don's explanation of his actions raised suspicions among investigators. It seemed odd that someone who had just witnessed the brutal murder of his family would be more concerned with changing his clothing than seeking immediate help or ensuring his own safety, especially if the attacker might still be nearby.

Investigators also noticed several small scratches on Don's neck. When asked about these, Don claimed he and Marthella had fought a few hours before the killings but couldn't remember what the fight was about.

Don told investigators that after changing his shirt, he had returned to the barn to hide for a few minutes in case the attackers came back. He then got into his father's truck, stopped at the gate to pick up the guns, informed the workers about the attack, and continued the five-mile drive to the police station.

Something Don mentioned didn't sit well with detectives. If he had found the murder weapons near the gate and no other guns were missing, why did he hear more gunshots coming from the house as he drove away? And if the killer was still in the house, why hadn't they crossed paths?

Another odd detail in Don's story was his claim of being in the barn when the attack began, yet he hadn't heard a vehicle approaching, and the four dogs hadn't barked. Had the killer arrived on foot? If so, how did they escape?

Additionally, investigators knew that after Marthella was shot the first time, she fled to a tree outside, where she was shot again. This tree was just a few feet from the barn, yet Don mentioned nothing of this in his account.

Investigators also questioned why Don hadn't armed himself or called the police rather than driving to the station. Another issue arose with his story about the t-shirt. Experts doubted that Marthella, in her weakened state, could have torn his shirt as he claimed.

As investigators delved more into the case, they discovered problems with Don's explanation of the timing of events. Don had arrived at the police station at 6:50 p.m. However, he had no way of knowing that his mother had sent a text message to Marthella at 6:34 p.m., indicating she was alive at that time. It would have been impossible for Don to hide in the barn for fifteen minutes, go into the house to watch his sister die in his arms, change his shirt, return to the barn for a few more minutes, pick up the two guns near the gate, warn the farm workers, and drive five miles to the police station—all in just sixteen minutes.

However, investigators soon found answers to all their questions when the forensic analysis of Don's t-shirt was completed. The shirt tested positive for gunshot residue and had distinct patterns of blood spatter. If Don had held his sister in his arms as he claimed, the blood would have been smeared, not spattered. This evidence made it clear that fifteen-year-old Don Steenkamp had killed his own family.

The rape of his younger sister, Marthella, was Don's clear motive. Investigators believed he had sexually assaulted his own sister and then killed his family to cover up what he had done.

Investigators later discovered incriminating text messages between Don and one of his friends in the hours after the murders.

Who do they suspect?

Only me.

Are there no other fingerprints?

No, only mine.

Is there no other evidence to find someone else?

No. They're not going to find anyone else.

On August 21, 2012, four months after the brutal killings, Don Steenkamp was handcuffed and arrested at his school in front of his classmates. He was charged with three counts of murder, defeating the ends of justice, and the sexual assault of his sister Marthella. He pleaded not guilty to all five charges.

The following month, Don Steenkamp was granted bail to continue attending school. His classmates and teachers recalled that before the murders, he had been quiet and reserved. However, after the murders, his demeanor changed dramatically. He relished the newfound attention, especially from girls; he became outgoing, with many describing him as arrogant.

However, many parents were anxious and outraged. They voiced their objections to the school administration, insisting that allowing an accused triple murderer to attend classes alongside their children was unacceptable. Ultimately, the school's administration decided that Don's presence was too disruptive and asked him to leave.

Before the trial began, the Northern Cape High Court agreed to release 500,000 South African Rand (approximately USD 60,000) from Don's inheritance from his grandfather to pay for his defense. However, the court did not permit the use of any funds from the USD 1.2 million that would have come from his deceased parents' estates.

In 1969, South Africa abolished the jury system, leaving the responsibility of determining a defendant's guilt solely in the hands of the presiding judge.

Don Steenkamp was seventeen when his trial began in 2014, two years after the murders.

The prosecution's case was built on circumstantial evidence, as there were no witnesses to the crimes. They presented evidence that Marthella had been raped between twelve and twenty-four hours before her death and highlighted inconsistencies in Don's version of events and the timeline he provided. Bloodstain analysis from his t-shirt indicated that Don was in close proximity to his sister when she was shot. They also pointed to text messages between Don and his friend shortly after the murders, suggesting he was confident no other evidence would be found.

The defense argued that the prosecution's case was purely circumstantial, lacking concrete proof linking Don to the crimes. They suggested that Marthella's sexual assault injuries could have been self-inflicted or caused by bareback horseback riding. Don Steenkamp testified in his own defense, claiming that an unknown intruder had committed the murders. However, his demeanor during the testimony was perceived as emotionless and arrogant.

During testimony, a psychologist who had spoken to Don revealed that, the day after the killings, one of Don's first concerns was how his inheritance would be worked out. Don mentioned that he knew how much he was set to inherit and noted that he would now also inherit Marthella's portion.

After several weeks of trial, the judge returned a guilty verdict on all counts. The judge stated that, based on the evidence presented, he was convinced it was not the first time Don had raped his younger sister.

In his final statement, the judge said,

> "I am satisfied that no one other than the minor accused, committed all the offenses listed in the indictment, as the state has, in fact, proved them. Not only beyond a reasonable doubt, but beyond any shadow of a doubt.

> To deal with all aspects proved against the minor would amount to an overkill.
>
> The murders were not only premeditated, but were, in fact, planned and executed with the direct intent to murder.
>
> In my view, the minor, the torturer, wanted to have sexual intercourse with Marthella. When she refused, she was consequently tortured, raped, and murdered; to prevent her from reporting it.
>
> Her parents had to be eliminated.
>
> There would be no reason for Marthella to inform anyone of the sexual activity if a consensual love relationship existed between her and the accused.
>
> The truth is, he is the architect of his own misfortune. He is the one who raised the alarm with the police and cried wolf."

Just two days before his eighteenth birthday, Don Steenkamp was sentenced to twelve years for the rape of Marthella, twenty years for each of the three murders, and four years for defeating the ends of justice. The sentences would run concurrently, resulting in a total sentence of twenty years.

As he was taken from the courtroom, Don Steenkamp hugged several family members, including his grandmother, who told television reporters that she accepted the verdict and believed he was guilty, but she still loved and forgave him, stating that Don would always be her sweet little boy.

Don Steenkamp becomes eligible for parole in 2024. However, even if granted parole, it is improbable that he will gain access to his family's inheritance without a successful appeal. This is due to South Africa's legal principle known as "bloedige hand" (bloody hand), which precludes an individual from inheriting as a beneficiary of their own criminal actions.

CHAPTER 4
HARVARD TRAINED

Amy Bishop grew up in the early 1970s in Braintree, Massachusetts, acutely aware of her own uniqueness. Her father, Sam, a professor of art at Northeastern University, and her mother, Judy, an elected town council member with influence over the town's budget, provided Amy with a privileged and intellectually stimulating upbringing.

As a child, Amy faced the challenges of severe asthma and allergies, conditions that often led to frequent hospitalizations. These chronic health issues sparked a deep passion for science in her early years, driving her determination to find a cure and alleviate the suffering of others. Throughout her high school years, Amy dedicated herself to her studies; her diligence yielded impressive results.

However, despite her intelligence and academic prowess, Amy often found herself overshadowed by her younger brother, Seth. While Amy had to work diligently for her achievements, Seth's successes seemed to come effortlessly. This apparent disparity in their natural abilities became a source of frustration and resentment for Amy as she grew older.

Seth's personality was a stark contrast to Amy's. He was personable and well-liked by both peers and teachers, possessing a natural charm and ease in social situations. Seth easily made friends, drawing people in with his friendly demeanor and engaging presence.

On the other hand, Amy was awkward and nerdy. She struggled to connect with others and often came across as socially inept.

Seth was a prodigy in both mathematics and science, and his natural abilities placed him head and shoulders above his peers. Determined not to be overshadowed, Amy took up the violin and quickly displayed a remarkable musical talent. However, Seth soon followed in her footsteps, and to Amy's dismay, he not only matched her skill but surpassed it, proving himself a true virtuoso.

It seemed that whatever Amy could do, Seth could do better. He excelled in areas where she struggled, effortlessly charming friends and impressing teachers with his brilliance. Seth's accolades were numerous and varied: he became a member of the prestigious Boston Youth Symphony, held the title of concertmaster in their high school orchestra, won the coveted National High School Math Award, and swept both the chemistry and biology categories in science competitions.

As if that weren't enough, Seth's literary talents were also recognized when their high school magazine published several of his short stories. For Amy, living in the shadow of her younger brother's achievements was a constant challenge. She felt the pressure to measure up to his successes, knowing that he had set a daunting standard for her to follow. The fact that Seth was her junior only added to Amy's frustration and sense of inadequacy.

After graduating high school, Amy enrolled at Northeastern University, where she crossed paths with the man who would eventually become her husband, Jimmy Anderson. However, Amy took issue with his name, believing that an adult going by the moniker "Jimmy" came across as unsophisticated and low-class. In her mind, the name lacked the refinement and professionalism she sought in a partner.

Determined to elevate his image, Amy insisted on addressing him as "James," a more distinguished and mature-sounding alternative. She made this decision unilaterally, disregarding the fact that Jimmy's legal name was, in fact, Jimmy.

Three years later, Seth followed in his sister's footsteps and also enrolled in Northeastern University, but the tension between brother and sister had only intensified.

On December 9, 1986, twenty-one-year-old Amy retrieved a shotgun her father had purchased the previous year after their house had been burglarized. Amy pulled the gun from her father's closet, took it to her bedroom, loaded it, and blew a hole in her bedroom wall. She then went downstairs to where her mother and brother were, aimed the gun at Seth, and shot him in the chest.

Amy's mother rushed to the aid of her son while Amy, still gripping the shotgun tightly, fled through the back door and ran down the alley behind their home.

At one point, Amy saw a car and pointed the gun at it, ordering the driver to get out. But the driver didn't stop and just kept going. Amy then made her way to a Ford car dealership nearby. However, it was after hours, and the dealership was already closed.

Panic-stricken and desperate, Amy frantically tried to open the doors of the parked cars, hoping she would find one with the keys left inside. Her erratic behavior caught the attention of three mechanics who were working late. As they approached the young woman, they noticed the shotgun in her hands, causing two of them to run in fear.

Amy, her mind racing, pointed the shotgun at the lone mechanic and demanded he get the keys to one of the vehicles. She lied, claiming she had just been involved in a violent altercation with her husband, who was now chasing her. Pleading with the mechanic, she insisted she needed to escape—otherwise, her husband would kill her.

The mechanic, raising his hands in surrender, calmly explained that he didn't have access to any car keys. Moments later, a police officer arrived on the scene and immediately drew his weapon, ordering Amy to drop the shotgun. However, still gripped by fear and desperation, Amy refused to back down.

As the tense standoff continued, a second officer managed to approach Amy from behind, his gun pointed at her head from point-blank range. With a firm voice, he commanded her to drop the shotgun.

Finally realizing the futility of her situation, Amy released her grip on the weapon, which was still loaded with one shell in the chamber, meaning Amy had to have racked its slide after shooting her brother. A search revealed she had another shell in her pocket.

Eighteen-year-old Seth was rushed to the hospital, but despite the efforts of medical staff, his injuries proved too severe to overcome. The shotgun blast had torn through his chest, causing catastrophic damage. Seth died within a few hours.

During a brief investigation of the incident, Amy's mother, an influential city council member with close ties to local law enforcement, provided a different explanation of events. She claimed that Amy had accidentally fired the gun while cleaning it. Surprisingly, no charges were filed against Amy, and Seth's death was officially ruled an accident. Sadly, the truth would remain hidden for twenty-five years.

Amy Bishop took no time off from school after Seth's death. The following August, she married Jimmy Anderson in the same church where her brother's funeral had been held just nine months earlier. Determined to make a name for herself, Amy kept her Bishop surname. Respecting her wishes, Jimmy promised to no longer go by Jimmy in public.

Amy graduated cum laude in 1988 with a degree in biology after submitting her honors thesis titled "The Effect of Temperature on the Recovery of Sea Lamprey from Full Spinal Cord Transection."

With her sights set on even greater heights, Amy moved on to Harvard University. As she pored herself into her doctoral studies, she and Jimmy had their first three children, all daughters, juggling the demands of parenthood and academia.

In 1993, Amy's hard work and dedication paid off as she earned her Ph.D. in genetics. Eager to continue her research, she secured a postdoctoral position at the prestigious neurobiology lab at Children's Hospital in Boston. However, during this time, her relationship with her supervisor, Dr. Paul Rosenberg, began to unravel.

Dr. Rosenberg expressed concerns about Amy's performance, indicating that he intended to give her a negative evaluation. He felt she wasn't meeting the rigorous standards required for the work. It was a heavy blow to Amy's ego and ambitions. To make matters worse, Amy struggled to maintain positive relationships with her colleagues, frequently engaging in heated arguments and displaying her volatile temper.

One particularly incendiary incident occurred when Amy collaborated with several other scientists on a research paper. When she discovered that her name was not listed first among the authors, Amy flew into a rage, her anger and frustration palpable to those around her.

As November 1993 drew to a close, Amy found herself seething over the impending negative evaluation from Dr. Rosenberg. Her coworkers noticed a marked change in her demeanor, describing her as on the verge of a nervous breakdown. Feeling cornered and unable to cope with the mounting pressure, Amy hastily submitted her resignation. Jimmy Anderson told a colleague he, too, was so angry that he wanted to "shoot, stab, or strangle" Dr. Rosenberg.

Less than a month had passed when Dr. Paul Rosenberg received a suspicious package on his doorstep. Alarmed by its unusual appearance and lack of return address, he immediately contacted the police.

As the police cautiously opened the box, their worst fears were confirmed. Inside the unassuming package lay two menacing pipe bombs, each six inches in length and rigged to nine-volt batteries. Acting swiftly, the bomb squad skillfully disarmed the explosives, meticulously preserving any evidence that could lead to the person responsible for the delivery.

When asked about potential suspects who might harbor such intense anger toward him, Dr. Rosenberg's thoughts immediately turned to Dr. Amy Bishop.

Armed with this information, the police wasted no time in converging on the home of Amy Bishop and her husband, Jimmy Anderson. The couple, however, refused to answer the door, and officers forced their way in through a window.

Once inside, the police meticulously combed through the couple's belongings, searching for any evidence that could link them to the pipe bombs. They collected photographs and fingerprints, hoping to find a match that would conclusively prove Bishop and Anderson's involvement in the crime.

The box containing the bombs was traced back to a box of Avery notepads, identical to those found in their home. Investigators also discovered a receipt from a nearby store listing purchases of an electrical switch, screws, guns, and black powder—items similar to those used in the bombs. However, these specific items were not found in the house during the search.

Despite their thorough investigation, authorities were unable to uncover concrete evidence linking the couple to the attempted bombing. Lacking sufficient proof to proceed, no charges were filed against Amy Bishop or Jimmy Anderson, leaving the case frustratingly unresolved.

Amy Bishop's time at Harvard University had a profound impact on her sense of self, shaping her identity and the way she presented herself to the world. After completing her doctoral studies and earning the coveted title of "Dr.," Amy made sure that everyone she encountered knew of her academic pedigree. She took every opportunity to introduce herself as "Dr. Amy Bishop—Harvard trained," emphasizing her connection to the prestigious institution and the rigorous education she had received.

However, despite her impressive credentials, Amy struggled to maintain stable employment in the research field. She secured positions at various hospitals, eager to make her mark and contribute to groundbreaking discoveries. Yet, her tenure at each institution was often short-lived due to frequent conflicts with colleagues.

Amy Bishop briefly pursued writing fiction, producing three unpublished novels whose characters closely paralleled her own life experiences. One novel depicted a character profoundly impacted by the loss of his brother. Another novel centered on a female researcher grappling with career frustrations and yearning for tenure—a reflection of Amy's own aspirations and challenges in the research field.

In 2001, on her late brother Seth's birthday, Amy gave birth to their fourth child, a boy they named Seth. Many who knew her found it strange and disturbing that Amy chose to name her child after the brother she had killed years earlier.

In March 2002, the family visited an IHOP restaurant in Peabody, Massachusetts. When Amy requested a booster seat for Seth, the waitress informed her that the last one had been given to another family nearby. While this might seem like a minor inconvenience to most people, it was completely unacceptable to Amy.

Amy approached the mother of the family who had taken the last booster seat and demanded that she give it to her. When the woman refused, Amy screamed, "Do you know who I am? I am Dr. Amy Bishop!" and punched the woman in the head. The restaurant staff quickly called the police, and Amy was arrested and charged with assault. She later pleaded guilty to the charge and received probation. Although prosecutors recommended anger management classes, Amy did not attend any.

In 2003, Amy was offered the position of associate professor of biology at the University of Alabama in Huntsville. In her new position, Amy and her husband invented a new kind of automated cell incubator.

As an Associate Professor, Amy was eligible to earn tenure. Tenure grants faculty members, such as professors or researchers, permanent positions at the institution, providing job security and protection from easy dismissal.

Tenure is typically granted after a probationary period, during which the faculty member's teaching, research, and service contributions are evaluated. If the faculty member meets the institution's standards for excellence, they may be awarded tenure.

However, students at the university saw two sides to Amy Bishop. Some saw her as a brilliant academic, while others found her obsessed with bragging about her Harvard degree.

Reviews from her students on RateMyProfessor.com stated:

> "...aloof and arrogant."
>
> "Dr. Bishop is very unclear in her test preparation, grading, and overall teaching style. She's not at all organized, and neither are her lab instructors. The tests are relatively easy, and you never really have to go to class except on review day."
>
> "For a Harvard graduate, she has very little common sense."

Other students remarked that Amy Bishop frequently read directly from textbooks without adding her own insights or elaborating on details. There were also complaints that tests sometimes covered material not discussed in class. Additionally, she was known to compare her students unfavorably to those at Harvard, suggesting they weren't as intelligent.

Her students disliked her so much that some began a petition to have her removed from the university. The petition was hand-delivered to the head of the biological sciences program, but the request was quickly ignored.

For a time, the university was willing to overlook the student complaints as long as her research and papers could bring in grant money. Amy's work on her cell incubation had brought the university more than $1 million in grants, and she was confident she would be awarded tenure.

Over the span of five years, however, Amy had published only three papers in relatively small publications. Her third paper was published in a "vanity press," where an author can pay to have almost anything published. However, the paper listed her husband and three young daughters as co-authors and was later retracted.

After completing her fifth year at the University of Alabama in Huntsville, Amy Bishop submitted her application for tenure. The application would undergo several reviews to assess her suitability. If she didn't receive tenure by the end of her sixth year, her employment would be terminated.

When her tenure was denied after a thorough review, Amy was outraged. However, she wasn't about to give up. Amy appealed the decision, alleging discrimination because one of the reviewers had referred to her as "crazy." Despite being given the opportunity to retract the comment, the reviewing professor refused.

> "I said she was crazy multiple times, and I stand by that. This woman has a pattern of erratic behavior. She did things that weren't normal. She was out of touch with reality."

Frustrated and livid, Amy hired a lawyer to assist with her appeal, but it was clear the university was finished with her. In early February 2010, the University of Alabama in Huntsville informed Amy that her final appeal had been denied and her employment would be terminated after she finished the semester.

Amy Bishop felt a boiling anger within her as her entire life's work crumbled around her. Yet, the school still expected her to continue teaching her classes for the remainder of the semester.

On February 12, Amy taught her two classes for the day: Introduction to Neuroscience and Anatomy and Physiology. Following her second class, Amy drove home to have lunch with Jimmy. According to Jimmy, the lunch seemed normal.

After lunch, Jimmy drove Amy back to the school for a faculty meeting. Amy felt irritated that she had to attend, knowing she wouldn't be there for the next semester. During the drive, she and Jimmy talked about their plans for a date night after the faculty meeting.

The faculty meeting was held on the third floor of the Shelby Center for Science and Technology, and Amy Bishop remained silent. She sat near the door for forty minutes until the meeting finished at 3:37 p.m.

Just as the meeting adjourned, Amy stood, reached into her purse, and pulled out a Ruger P89 nine-millimeter semi-automatic pistol. She started with the person closest to her, Dr. Gopi Podila, an Indian-American biologist who was chairman of the biology department. She shot him execution-style in the head. She then went down the right side of the oval conference table and continued shooting. Dr. Maria Ragland Davis and Dr. Adriel D. Johnson Sr., both associate professors, were shot at point-blank range.

The room erupted into chaos as the other nine attendees scrambled for safety, some fleeing for the door while others sought cover under tables. Amy, with a cold stare, fired at two more biology professors and a staff assistant. However, when she aimed the gun at biochemistry professor Dr. Debra Moriarty, it either jammed or she had run out of ammunition—only a click followed.

Debra Moriarty had thought of Amy Bishop as a friend, but she quickly took the pause in mayhem as an opportunity to rush Amy. She pleaded with Amy not to shoot and tried to restrain her arms. Dr. Moriarty then fled from the conference room with Amy in pursuit. She was still trying to fire the gun.

Unable to locate Dr. Moriarty in the hallways, Amy eventually returned to the conference room, where the remaining attendees had barricaded themselves inside. Dr. Cruz-Vera, struggling from a gaping gunshot wound to his chest, urgently called 911 for help.

Amy Bishop hurried down a stairwell to a restroom on the second floor. There, she wrapped her gun in her jacket, placed it in a garbage can, and covered it with paper towels. After leaving the restroom, she flagged down a passing student and borrowed their cell phone to call her husband.

With a sudden calmness in her voice, Amy told Jimmy he could pick her up now—the meeting was over.

Students had been evacuated from the building, and officers had already found the murder weapon in the second-floor bathroom, but they hadn't found Amy Bishop.

When Jimmy arrived to pick her up minutes later, he found the area swarming with police cars, completely unaware that his wife had just gone on a rampage and shot six people.

Police cleared the building, and emergency workers rushed to the conference room. Dr. Gopi Podila, Dr. Maria Ragland Davis, and Dr. Adriel Johnson were tragically pronounced dead at the scene. Dr. Luis Cruz-Vera, Dr. Joseph Leahy, and Stephanie Monticciolo were rushed to the hospital and eventually recovered from their injuries.

Amy Bishop was apprehended by police as she emerged from a door on the school's loading dock. Jimmy Anderson watched in shock as his wife shook her head and muttered,

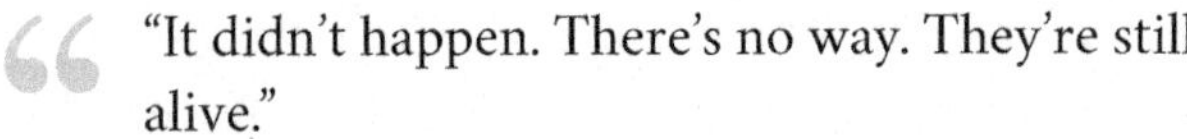

> "It didn't happen. There's no way. They're still alive."

During the initial investigation, detectives interviewed Jimmy Anderson, who claimed he saw no indication that his wife would commit such an act. However, he conveniently omitted that Amy had previously shot and killed her younger brother, was suspected of sending a pipe bomb to the home of her former lab supervisor, and had assaulted a woman at an IHOP. Although he admitted to owning a gun, he failed to mention that he and Amy had recently gone target shooting with the same gun she used in the fatal shooting of three people.

After Amy Bishop was arrested, some people at the university were worried that she might have hidden a "herpes bomb" in the science building to spread the virus. This concern came up because Amy had studied the herpes virus during her postdoctoral research and had even written a novel about a virus like herpes spreading across the world. Police, however, searched the building and found nothing.

During her interrogation, Amy insisted she wasn't present at the faculty meeting on the day of the shooting. She stuck to her claim despite all ten people who were there identifying her as the shooter.

During the search of Amy Bishop and Jimmy Anderson's home, investigators seized computers, a video camera, and documents pertaining to Amy's legal disputes with the university. They also discovered a piece of pipe that matched the one used in the attempted bombing of Dr. Rosenberg seventeen years earlier. Despite this finding, bomb squads found no explosives on the property.

Although investigators still believed that she and Jimmy could have been responsible for making and delivering the bomb, they couldn't prove that the couple actually made or delivered the bomb to Dr. Rosenberg, and the case remained cold.

When news of Amy Bishop's rampage reached the chief of police in her hometown of Braintree, Massachusetts, he promptly contacted the Huntsville police. He relayed that Amy had shot and killed her younger brother in 1986 amidst rumors that the previous chief of police had brushed the case under the rug, allowing Amy to avoid arrest.

The new police chief managed to locate the original case files related to Seth Bishop's death. These files had been mysteriously hidden away at the home of a police captain who had long since passed away.

Upon reviewing the rediscovered documents, a more detailed and disturbing picture of the events following Seth's shooting emerged. The files revealed that Amy Bishop had not simply fled the scene after shooting her brother but had actively threatened others with the shotgun as she made her escape.

The discovery of these hidden files raised serious questions about the initial handling of the case and the decision not to press charges against Amy Bishop. It also highlighted the need for a thorough re-examination of the evidence and a more comprehensive investigation into Seth Bishop's death. Former police chief John Polio, who was now eighty-seven, denied any cover-up of the crime.

The original police file, however, clearly indicated that Amy's mother's account of an accidental shooting was highly unlikely. Amy had taken four rounds of ammunition from her father's bedroom. After firing a shot into the wall of her bedroom, she racked the gun, ejected the spent shell casing, and reloaded it. She then proceeded downstairs and shot her brother. After killing him, she racked and reloaded the gun again before leaving the house.

The discovery of the hidden case files also raised questions about the credibility of Judy Bishop's initial statements to police.

Judy Bishop had claimed that she was present when Amy accidentally shot Seth. She had provided a timeline of events suggesting that she witnessed the shooting firsthand and that it was an unintentional act.

After interviewing several officers and detectives who remembered the 1986 shooting, many believed the killing was not accidental; former Chief Polio and Judy Bishop were friends and had covered the crime up.

Even if there were doubts surrounding the death of Seth Bishop, Amy had held people up at gunpoint and easily could have been charged with assault with a dangerous weapon, carrying a dangerous weapon, and unlawful possession of ammunition.

During an inquest in March 2010, Braintree officers testified that they were ordered to release Amy Bishop after her mother had asked explicitly to speak to Chief Polio, whom she considered a friend.

In June 2010, a grand jury indicted Amy for the first-degree murder of her brother twenty-four years after the incident. Two days after the indictment, Amy slashed her wrists with a razor blade in her cell, but she was promptly treated for the wound. The following month, she was formally charged with first-degree murder.

After the shooting in Huntsville, Amy Bishop was charged with one count of capital murder and three counts of attempted murder. Prosecutors initially indicated they would seek the death penalty. However, after conversations with the families of the victims and survivors, none of them wanted a death sentence for Amy Bishop.

Amy Bishop's legal team initially planned to pursue an insanity defense, given her assertion that she had no memory of the shooting. They believed that her claimed lack of recollection could potentially support an argument that she was not mentally sound at the time of the crime.

However, the fact that Amy had actively tried to hide the gun after the shooting posed a significant challenge to this defense strategy. Her attempt to hide the weapon indicated an awareness of her actions and an understanding that what she had done was wrong. Amy's lawyers realized that an insanity plea would face significant hurdles in court.

Recognizing the uphill battle they were facing, Amy and her legal team changed her plea to guilty in exchange for the prosecution agreeing not to seek the death penalty. The prosecution, however, had one stipulation—she had to waive her right to appeal.

On September 24, 2012, Amy Bishop pled guilty to one count of capital murder and three counts of attempted murder. She was sentenced to life in prison without the possibility of parole.

Given Amy Bishop's life sentence in Alabama, Norfolk County, Massachusetts, declined to seek extradition to try her for her brother's murder.

Despite waiving her right to appeal, Amy Bishop appealed her conviction in 2013, claiming she didn't understand her rights. Her appeal was quickly denied.

In 2021, Amy's twenty-year-old son, Seth Anderson, was accidentally shot and killed by a friend who reportedly mishandled a gun.

CHAPTER 5
THE DEMON

Nestled on England's western coast, Blackpool has drawn visitors for over a century. Its vibrant waterfront, iconic roller coaster park, 518-foot tower, and lively Light Festival make it a beloved summer getaway in the UK.

Just four miles inland from Blackpool's bustling promenade lies the tranquil village of Staining. With a population of just over 2,000, Staining appeared to be an idyllic haven for raising a family.

In 2004, Jane and Gary Marsden relocated to Staining with their five children, including eight-year-old Sasha. Growing up in this small town, Sasha was known for her infectious humor, sociability, and mischievous spirit. She had a knack for making others laugh and an insatiable passion for dancing. Sasha would often break into spontaneous dance moves wherever she heard music, turning ordinary moments into lively, unforgettable experiences for her friends and family.

As Sasha entered her teenage years, she and her friends gravitated toward the vibrant energy of Blackpool, preferring its lively attractions over the quiet village life of Staining. They frequently took the bus to town, strolling along the promenade and relishing the thrills of the Pleasure Beach amusement park.

In the summer of 2010, shortly after turning fourteen, Sasha and a friend hopped on a bus bound for Blackpool, eager for a day of beachside fun.

Sasha had promised her mother she'd be home by 9:00 p.m., so Jane Marsden wasn't surprised when the phone rang at 8:30. She anticipated Sasha pleading to stay out a bit longer. However, Jane was taken aback when she realized it wasn't her daughter on the line—it was Blackpool police.

Jane's initial fear was that her daughter had encountered trouble with the law. However, what the police told her was far more devastating.

Earlier that evening, police reported that Sasha and her friend had been in a public park where a twenty-two-year-old man initiated a conversation with them. As they chatted, the man befriended them and eventually offered to share a bottle of vodka.

At just fourteen, Sasha, thin and petite, wasn't accustomed to drinking alcohol and quickly recoiled from its sharp taste. The man laughed it off, assuring her she'd grow accustomed to it. Before long, Sasha became intoxicated and eventually passed out in the park.

In broad daylight and in front of Sasha's young friend, the man undressed Sasha and sexually assaulted her. Her friend, a thirteen-year-old boy, had tried to pull the man off, but he was far too little and no match for the attacker.

Determined to help, the boy cried out, piercing the evening air and drawing the attention of two nearby women. Startled by the urgency in his voice, they hurried to the scene. With swift action, they managed to separate the man from Sasha, called the police, and held him down until authorities arrived.

The man was promptly arrested and later sentenced to five years and four months in prison. Despite justice being served, the traumatic incident left Sasha deeply scarred, its emotional impact casting a long shadow over her life.

Once vibrant and cheerful, Sasha became withdrawn and depressed following the incident. Coping became a daily struggle, often punctuated by sudden bursts of anger. She seemed a mere shadow of her former self.

Two weeks later, Sasha attempted to return to school, hoping for some semblance of normalcy. Instead, her classmates' reactions deepened her trauma. Rather than support her, some bullied her with derogatory names and rumors. Shockingly, someone even created a hurtful Facebook page dedicated to taunting Sasha, suggesting she deserved her ordeal.

As months passed, Sasha's appetite dwindled, and sleep became elusive, haunted by terrifying nightmares that left her in tears. Her once-vibrant confidence vanished, replaced by a deep sense of vulnerability and exposure.

The relentless bullying exacerbated Sasha's fragile mental state. She started skipping school often, unable to confront her tormentors. Despite transferring to another school in hopes of finding respite, Sasha continued to struggle, finding it challenging to adapt to her new environment.

Over time, Sasha's behavior spiraled into self-destructive patterns marked by heavy drinking and erratic actions. Her relationships with friends and family deteriorated as she frequently lashed out in anger over minor disagreements.

Sasha's excessive drinking also led to risky sexual behavior. Seeking control over her body and sexuality following her trauma, she engaged in multiple sexual relationships. Experts later noted that this attempt to cope ultimately damaged her sense of self-worth even further.

To avoid interference from her parents, Sasha began running away from home. In the span of one month, she disappeared on four separate occasions, leaving her family sick with worry each time. Her parents tirelessly searched around Blackpool, consumed by worry for their daughter. This pattern persisted for two years, coinciding with Sasha's worsening mental health.

In 2012, sixteen-year-old Sasha began dating a young man named Danny. Initially, her parents were apprehensive about the relationship. since Danny was two years older than Sasha. However, as their relationship progressed, they noticed positive changes in Sasha—signs of the bright, ambitious girl they once knew. Danny seemed to provide stability.

Danny even joined the Marsden family for dinner, briefly restoring a sense of normalcy. It appeared that Sasha was beginning to reclaim her former self. Then, on August 31, 2012, Sasha vanished once more. Calls to her cell phone went unanswered, and Danny was unreachable. Late that evening, Sasha's parents contacted the police, desperate to find their missing daughter.

Two days later, Sasha's parents anxiously awaited news, fearing the worst. Late that evening, their phone finally rang. To their surprise and relief, it was Sasha on the other end of the line. She wasn't in Blackpool anymore but 300 miles away in Lowestoft, on the opposite side of the United Kingdom.

Sasha explained that she and Danny had run away to start a new life together, and they had no intention of returning.

Her parents quickly persuaded the teenagers to return home. Jane and Gary offered a deal: if Sasha came back, they would support her and Danny, ensuring their safety by letting them live with them.

Upon Sasha and Danny's return to her parents' home in September 2012, a noticeable shift occurred in Sasha's life. The tumultuous two years marked by anger, self-destructive behavior, and runaway attempts seemed to give way to newfound stability and optimism. Danny's presence in the family home appeared to have a soothing influence on Sasha, prompting her parents to observe a significant improvement in her overall demeanor.

Encouraged by this positive change, Sasha decided to join a childcare course at Blackpool and The Fylde College. This decision marked a significant move toward a promising future and a career focused on working with children, an area Sasha had always been passionate about. As she started her studies, Sasha's innate talent for nurturing others became evident, and she soon flourished in the college setting.

Sasha's course involved practical placements at Blackpool's Victoria Hospital, where she gained hands-on experience caring for toddlers in the hospital's nursery.

Things were looking up for Sasha. She was getting along better with her parents, and her relationship with Danny was excellent. Even her parents were happy with the living arrangements.

In January 2013, an unexpected opportunity came Sasha's way when she received a Facebook message from a friend of a friend. The message offered her a part-time cleaning position at a small hotel in Blackpool. Sasha was thrilled by the chance to earn her own money, especially since the hours fit perfectly with her college schedule.

Initially concerned about their sixteen-year-old daughter working alone in hotel rooms, Jane and Gary Marsden expressed reservations. However, Sasha's enthusiasm and her reassurances that the hotel was owned by an acquaintance of her friend helped ease their concerns. After careful consideration and discussion, Sasha's parents agreed to let her take the job under the condition that her father would drop her off and pick her up from each shift.

As Sasha prepared for her upcoming interview and trial shift at the hotel, she couldn't help but feel a sense of pride and accomplishment in her journey. From a troubled teenager, she had grown into a young woman with a clear direction and purpose, eagerly embracing new challenges and opportunities that promised to shape a better future for herself.

On Monday, January 28, 2013, Gary Marsden dropped Sasha off at a corner in Blackpool. Uncertain of the exact location of the hotel, Sasha was informed by the man that they would meet near the seafront and walk to the hotel together.

Several hours later, Sasha called home to inform her parents that she was ready to be picked up. Gary met her at the same street corner, and Sasha eagerly got into the car, excited to share how things had gone. She told her father that the interview had gone very well. She explained that she'd had a chat with the manager over tea about her responsibilities. During the interview, she also cleaned a few rooms and made a few beds. The manager then paid her £10 for her time and confirmed that she could officially start the following Thursday.

On Thursday morning, Sasha went to college and received more good news. Her tutor praised her hard work and informed her that she would be advancing to the next level of her course.

That afternoon, Sasha's father drove her to the familiar spot near the hotel to drop her off. Once again, she assured him that she would text him when she finished her shift and was ready to come home. Gary kissed Sasha on the forehead, wished her good luck, and drove away.

Sasha was only scheduled to work a few hours and expected to be finished by 6:30 p.m. so she could be home for dinner with the family, but by 7:00, she hadn't called.

She and Danny had plans to see a movie at 8:00 that night, and they knew she wouldn't stand her boyfriend up. Still, 8:00 p.m. came and went with no contact from Sasha. Her parents tried calling and texting her, but her phone appeared to be switched off, which was highly out of character for the teenager.

When the family decided to search for her, it dawned on them that Sasha hadn't told them the name of the hotel where she was working. Gary had dropped her off near the shore, but there were dozens of small hotels in that area. They didn't know where to look.

Danny, however, had an idea. They knew Sasha had been hired by a man named David, who was a friend of a friend. Luckily, Danny had Sasha's Facebook password and logged into her account. There were only two contacts in her friends list named David. One was Danny's friend, and he knew it wasn't him. The other profile name was "David Demon Minto," and Sasha had only recently accepted his friend request days earlier. Looking through his Facebook photos, they found a picture of him standing in front of the Grafton House Hotel.

At 8:30 that evening, Jane and Gary Marsden arrived at the Grafton House Hotel and were greeted by twenty-two-year-old David Minto.

Minto told the Marsdens that Sasha had left hours ago, saying she was planning to meet her father near the waterfront. Sasha's parents, however, knew she wouldn't have left without contacting them first.

Worried sick, the Marsdens drove the streets of Blackpool looking for their daughter. They called hospitals and reached out to her friends on social media, but no one had heard from Sasha. By 11:00 that evening, Sasha's parents, in a state of panic, contacted the police to report her disappearance.

Fifteen minutes later, two police detectives arrived at the Marsden home and took down their description of Sasha. As the officers gathered information, one of them received a call and briefly left the room. Several minutes later, he re-entered the room with a look of despair on his face and sadly told Sasha's parents that they had reason to believe their daughter was dead.

Earlier that evening, Blackpool police officers had been called to an alleyway behind the Grafton House Hotel. A neighbor had noticed a fire in a dumpster in the alley and called other neighbors to help throw water on the flames. Initially, it appeared there was a mannequin burning at the bottom of the dumpster, but as the smoke cleared, one of the onlookers said, "Mannequins don't bleed."

David Minto had made the comment. Excited by the commotion, he ran back into the hotel to invite his girlfriend to come to the alley to see the burning body. David's girlfriend called the police.

When officers arrived, they found the badly burned body of a young girl wrapped in carpet and garbage bags. Her body was burned so badly that police were unable to identify her. The only clues to the victim's identity were the remnants of clothing - a burnt Adidas top, pink and white tennis shoes, and a pink handbag.

Later that night, however, when the detectives gathered Sasha's description from her parents, they immediately made the connection. The description of the clothing matched what Sasha had been wearing that day. Additionally, the location of the body, just behind the hotel where she had been working, was a tragic coincidence that could not be ignored.

Sasha had suffered fifty-eight stab wounds to the head, face, and neck. Defensive wounds on her hands and arms showed that she desperately tried to fight off her attacker. She had also been brutally sexually assaulted after her death.

By setting the body ablaze, the killer likely hoped to eliminate any physical traces of his involvement, such as DNA evidence or other incriminating materials.

On the other hand, the location and manner in which he chose to dispose of Sasha's body suggested a deeply disturbed individual seeking attention. The alleyway behind the hotel was situated in a busy area of Blackpool, and the killer would have been well aware that a fire in such a location would quickly draw the attention of nearby residents and passersby.

Blackpool police launched a full-scale investigation, treating Sasha's disappearance as a murder inquiry. Crime scene investigators meticulously combed the alleyway and the interior of the Grafton House Hotel for evidence.

They discovered significant amounts of blood in the hotel corridors, on the carpet, and in the bathtub of David Minto's living quarters. Bloodied pieces of Sasha's clothing, her mobile phone, and her purse were also found in the hotel.

Forensic experts found traces of Sasha's blood on a knife in the hotel kitchen, which was later determined to be the murder weapon. They also discovered Sasha's earrings and a necklace in the bathroom toilet, indicating that someone had attempted to flush them.

When Gary and Jane Marsden had spoken to David Minto on the doorstep of the Grafton House Hotel earlier that evening, they had no idea that their daughter's brutalized body was just steps away.

Detectives learned that while the Grafton House Hotel was owned by David Minto's girlfriend and her mother, Minto was the only person present when Sasha arrived for work that evening. Minto's girlfriend told detectives that when she returned to the hotel at around 9:00 that evening, she noticed a strong smell of bleach and cleaning products. David Minto told her he was cleaning up after a nosebleed.

She also told investigators that Minto only worked as a bartender and handyman and had no authority to hire anyone. Moreover, she explained there was no need to hire a cleaner since the hotel was closed for renovations and there were no guests.

Given the overwhelming forensic evidence linking Sasha's murder to the Grafton House Hotel, as well as David Minto's suspicious behavior and inconsistent statements, police arrested him on suspicion of murder.

During questioning, Minto told detectives that Sasha had made sexual advances toward him. He claimed they'd had consensual sex and that Sasha had a nosebleed shortly afterward, which he helped her clean up. Minto insisted that

Sasha had left the hotel alive and well, expressing shock and sadness upon learning of her death.

Three days later, however, with a mountain of physical evidence pointing toward him, David Minto was formally charged with Sasha Marsden's murder.

Six months after the murder, David Minto went on trial for murder and pleaded not guilty to the charges against him.

The prosecution argued that Minto had lured Sasha to the hotel under the pretense of a job opportunity, arranging for her to come on Monday and Thursday—days when he knew his girlfriend would be away at her other job.

They argued that Minto had planned to sexually assault the teenager, but when she had rejected his advances, he flew into a frenzied and sustained attack, stabbing her fifty-eight times in the head, face, and neck with a kitchen knife later found in the hotel.

The prosecution also contended that Minto had sexually defiled Sasha's body as she lay dying or already dead, and he had attempted to dispose of her remains by wrapping her body in carpet and garbage bags before setting it ablaze in the alleyway behind the hotel.

Throughout the trial, the jury was presented with a wealth of forensic evidence, including Sasha's blood found on Minto's clothing and throughout the hotel, as well as the murder weapon. Additionally, various witnesses testified, including a young woman who'd had a chilling encounter with David Minto just weeks before Sasha Marsden's death. The witness described how she had been lured to the

Grafton House Hotel by Minto under circumstances similar to those that tragically led to Sasha's fatal encounter with him.

While at the hotel, the young woman found herself in an uncomfortable situation when Minto began to make unsolicited and inappropriate sexual advances toward her. Fortunately, she was able to reject his attempts and managed to escape the hotel without suffering any physical harm.

The court learned that Sasha had only accepted Minto's friend request on January 27. He claimed to have known her through a mutual friend. She had no idea who he was but accepted his friend request out of politeness. Four days later, she was dead.

At trial, Minto's story had changed. His defense team still claimed that Sasha had made sexual advances toward him and they'd had consensual sex. However, she had left the hotel alive, and he'd continued his cleaning duties.

Shortly thereafter, they now explained, Minto found Sasha brutally murdered in the hotel by an unknown assailant. The defense claimed Minto then cleaned the crime scene and moved her body to the dumpster, where he burned it.

However, there was a gaping hole in the defense's theory. Upon finding Sasha's viciously stabbed body, a reasonable person's immediate response would be to alert the authorities and seek help, especially given the extreme violence of the crime and the clear indication that a homicidal maniac was inside the hotel.

Instead, Minto's reaction of attempting to clean the crime

scene and dispose of evidence suggests a far more incriminating involvement in the murder.

If Minto were truly an innocent bystander who had stumbled upon Sasha's lifeless body, his priority would have been to ensure his own safety and that of others by contacting the police immediately rather than engaging in a desperate attempt to cover up the crime.

After eleven days of trial, the jury deliberated for just three hours before returning a unanimous guilty verdict.

During sentencing, Judge Anthony Russell addressed Minto, stating, "There is not a shred of common humanity in you. You are, in my judgment, a very dangerous and evil man."

David Minto was sentenced to life in prison with a minimum term of thirty-five years. The Grafton House Hotel was closed permanently shortly after Sasha's murder.

Amidst the grief and pain that followed Sasha's untimely death, her sister Gemma channeled her energy into creating something positive and meaningful in her memory. She founded the Yes Matters charity, an organization dedicated to providing much-needed support to victims of abuse, and works tirelessly to shift societal attitudes surrounding critical issues such as consent, body image, and the way women are portrayed in the media.

CHAPTER 6
A KILLER BREAKTHROUGH

On a chilly Monday evening in late November 1983, fifteen-year-old Lynda Mann left her home to walk to a neighbor's house in the small village of Narborough, Leicestershire, England, to work for a few hours of babysitting.

As she had done many times before, she walked along a secluded footpath known as the Black Pad. It was a popular shortcut used by locals with tall trees and foliage on both sides of the lane. Generally, it was a safe way to quickly get from one side of the village to the other.

But when Lynda didn't arrive home by 10:00 p.m., her parents became worried. She should have been home long before. Panic set in when they called the home where she was supposed to be babysitting, but they learned Lynda had never arrived. Growing increasingly concerned for their daughter's safety, they called the police to report Lynda missing.

Lynda Mann was a bright and friendly young girl. By all accounts, she was a good-natured girl who was well-liked by her classmates. If police thought for a minute that she had run away, they were wrong.

Lynda's mother stayed up waiting for her daughter the entire night. In the morning, she still stood, looking out of the front window of their home and patiently hoping to see Lynda skipping down the sidewalk back toward home without a care in the world. Instead, she watched as two police officers walked up the steps toward her door.

When the officers asked her mother to sit down, she knew her world had just crumbled. That morning, a local man walking his dog along the Black Pad had discovered the partially clothed body of a young girl in a clump of bushes. She was hidden from view of the path, just a few hundred yards from her home.

Lynda Mann was found wearing only her bra, which had been pulled up. Her sweater, jeans, denim jacket, shoes, and underwear were found scattered around the crime scene. Her winter scarf was used as a ligature, tightly knotted around her neck.

Investigators believed the attacker had quickly overpowered the young girl since there was no evidence of a struggle or defensive wounds.

An autopsy revealed that Lynda had been raped and strangled to death with her own scarf. Semen was left on her body and clothing, but in 1983, DNA was unknown except within the scientific community and had never been used as a crime-solving tool. However, from the semen, they were able to determine the killer's blood type: type A. However, roughly ten percent of the male population had that blood type.

At Lynda's funeral, police videotaped the crowd, knowing that killers sometimes make themselves present at such events when a killing happens within a small-town setting, but the footage didn't provide any definitive clues.

The community of Narborough was deeply shaken by the crime. Many residents knew Lynda or her family personally, and the idea that such a brutal murder could happen in their quiet village was unthinkable. Parents watched their children closely, and women feared walking alone at night. The police launched a massive investigation, interviewing hundreds of potential witnesses and suspects, but after no solid leads emerged, the case eventually went cold.

Locals threw around theories, and many had speculated that the killer may have been a patient at a psychiatric hospital just a few hundred yards from where her body was found. However, there was no evidence to support that theory.

Three years had passed, and the Leicestershire police were no closer to solving Lynda Mann's murder. Lynda's friends and family were still grieving, but for many, life had returned to normal—until July 31, 1986.

On a Thursday afternoon, fifteen-year-old Dawn Ashworth left her part-time job at a local newsstand in Enderby, the village adjacent to Narborough, and began walking toward a friend's house. When she discovered her friend wasn't home, she tried another friend's house nearby, but she wasn't there either. Frustrated, Dawn headed toward home.

Dawn had two potential routes to walk home. One route would take her through populated residential streets and a busy main road, but that would take a little longer.

The second option was to take Ten Pound Lane, a secluded footpath lined with trees and bushes that served as a shortcut through the neighborhood and trimmed several minutes off her walk. It was a popular route she had taken many times before. The decision seemed innocuous at the time, but she had no way of knowing it would determine her fate.

As the late summer sun began to set, Dawn had not returned home. With each passing hour, her parents grew more frantic, eventually calling the police to report their daughter missing. Dawn had disappeared less than a mile from the location where Lynda Mann's body was found just three years earlier. Panic once again gripped the small villages.

Just two days later, on Saturday, August 2, Dawn Ashworth's body was found in a densely wooded area just off Ten Pound Lane, less than a half mile from the newsstand where she worked.

Dawn's naked body was found beneath leaves, branches, and grass clippings set back from the path. She had been violently raped with both a penis and an unknown object, then strangled to death with her bra. Her clothes had been ripped from her body and scattered nearby. Defensive wounds told investigators that Dawn had fought for her life. In addition to the strangulation, she had suffered blunt force trauma to her head and face, likely from being punched.

Like Lynda Mann's crime scene, the killer had left semen on her body and clothing. After analyzing the semen, investigators learned that Dawn Ashworth's killer had the same blood type as Lynda Mann's.

There were other similarities as well. Both girls were fifteen, lived in the same area, and were attacked on secluded footpaths. Both girls attended the same school, and both were brutally raped and strangled.

Once again, fear gripped the close-knit villages of Narborough, Enderby, and Littlethorpe. The towns were shocked and frightened that such a brutal crime could occur in their quiet, seemingly safe area.

Residents became suspicious of one another, and girls were terrified to leave the house alone. Police advised girls to walk in groups, and some began taking self-defense classes. Even pubs in the area were cleared out earlier than normal as people rushed home before nightfall.

The police diligently searched for the killer, going door-to-door and questioning nearby residents, but they still had no leads.

Investigators got their first break when a witness claimed to have seen a boy near Ten Pound Lane on the day of Dawn's murder.

Seventeen-year-old Richard Buckland lived in the vicinity of both murders and worked as a kitchen porter at the nearby Carlton Hayes Psychiatric Hospital.

Buckland was already known by police due to a string of previous convictions for minor sexual offenses. Detectives also noticed that Buckland had suspiciously been hanging around both murder scenes and had approached officers to ask how the investigation was progressing. He was also overheard saying that the police were looking in the wrong places for clues and that he believed the killer was a local man.

Based on his criminal history, strange behavior, and seemingly incriminating statements, detectives brought Buckland in for questioning on August 8, 1986. During the interrogation, Buckland shocked investigators by confessing to the murder of Dawn Ashworth. However, he adamantly denied any involvement in the earlier killing of Lynda Mann.

During his confession, Buckland revealed specific details about the crime scene that had not been made public, such as the clothing Dawn was wearing and the position of her body when it was discovered. This solidified their belief that he was Dawn's killer. However, one thing bothered detectives. They were convinced that both girls had been murdered by the same man, yet Buckland insisted he hadn't killed Lynda. Regardless, Buckland was arrested and charged with Dawn Ashworth's murder.

For several months, police tirelessly tried to connect Buckland to both crimes. Investigators enlisted the help of Dr. Alec Jeffreys, a genetics researcher at the nearby University of Leicester. Jeffreys had been researching hereditary diseases when he inadvertently developed a new technique called genetic fingerprinting—what we know today as DNA.

Investigators gave Jeffreys the semen samples from both murder cases, hoping to link Buckland to the crimes. However, the DNA results surprised the detectives. The tests did reveal that the same man was responsible for both murders, but Buckland was innocent; he hadn't murdered either girl. After spending four months in custody, Richard

Buckland became the first person in history to be exonerated by DNA evidence.

The reasons behind Buckland's false confession are still unclear. Some experts believe that his limited intellectual capacity, coupled with the intense pressure of the police interrogation, may have caused him to confess to a crime he didn't commit. Additionally, Buckland, who had a history of attention-seeking behavior, might have falsely confessed in a misguided effort to gain attention in the high-profile case.

Armed with the new DNA technology, investigators sent thousands of letters to every male between the ages of thirteen and thirty-three living in the three villages of Narborough, Littlethorpe, and Enderby.

The letters requested that they voluntarily report to mobile testing sites set up in the village halls and community centers to supply blood and saliva samples.

Over the next six months, more than 5,000 men voluntarily provided samples. While some were concerned about the reliability of the new technology and others worried about potential privacy violations, the vast majority of local men participated. Many viewed it as their civic duty to help catch the killer and restore safety to the community.

However, one individual did anything he could to avoid the DNA dragnet—twenty-seven-year-old Colin Pitchfork. Pitchfork, a married father of two boys, had been questioned by police earlier during the murder investigations due to his prior indecent exposure convictions.

In 1977, when he was just seventeen, Pitchfork exposed himself to a young girl. He pleaded guilty and was fined £30. Two years later, he sexually assaulted a sixteen-year-old girl. At twenty, he exposed himself to two young girls and received a year of probation. Three years later, Lynda Mann was raped and strangled.

When Pitchfork learned of the new DNA fingerprint technology, he knew that if he were tested, he would be caught.

Colin Pitchfork worked as a baker, and when he received the letter requesting blood samples from all males, he asked a coworker for a favor. Ian Kelly, who also worked at the same bakery, lived outside the area and hadn't received a letter.

Pitchfork lied to Kelly, telling him he had already submitted his own sample on behalf of another friend who didn't want to be harassed for his past criminal record. He then asked Kelly to take the test on his behalf.

In an elaborate ruse, Pitchfork meticulously removed his photo from his passport and substituted it with a photo of Ian Kelly. He then drove Kelly to a testing site and waited in the car while Kelly submitted the blood sample under Pitchfork's name. The plan worked flawlessly, and Colin Pitchfork's name was removed from the list of potential suspects.

The DNA dragnet ended in the spring of 1987, and Colin Pitchfork was reveling in successfully getting away with murder. However, that August, Ian Kelly was out with coworkers for a night of drinking at The Clarendon, a local pub.

After a few too many pints, Kelly was bragging to a friend about his involvement in providing a false DNA sample on Colin Pitchfork's behalf during the police's mass screening. Kelly's loose lips caught the attention of a woman who overheard the conversation. Realizing the gravity of the information and its potential implications for the ongoing murder investigation, the woman took it upon herself to report what she had heard to the police.

Detectives investigated the woman's tip and brought Ian Kelly in for questioning. Kelly quickly admitted to the deception and told detectives that Colin Pitchfork had asked him to provide the false sample.

When Colin Pitchfork was arrested on September 19, 1987, he initially denied any involvement in the murders of Lynda Mann and Dawn Ashworth. However, when confronted with the evidence of his fraudulent DNA sample and the fact that his genetic profile would be compared to the semen found on the victims, Pitchfork realized that he had no choice but to confess. During his interrogation, he provided the police with a detailed account of his crimes.

Pitchfork told detectives he had encountered Lynda Mann by chance after dropping his wife off at an evening class. His infant son had been in the car with him when he parked near the Black Pad footpath. Leaving his son alone in the car, he raped and murdered Lynda, then drove home as if nothing had happened.

Pitchfork said he had been out driving when he noticed Dawn Ashworth walking alone along Ten Pound Lane in Enderby. He followed her down the footpath and attacked her in a nearby field.

During the interrogation, Pitchfork also admitted to attacking another young woman nine months before Dawn Ashworth's murder. He had attacked and sexually assaulted the sixteen-year-old while threatening her with a screwdriver, but he had let her live.

He had also intended to attack another young girl, Liz Knight, while he was traveling. He gave the girl a ride in his car, but when she grabbed the wheel, he changed his mind. Instead, he drove her home. As he dropped her off, he said, "How about a good night kiss?" When she scoffed and walked away, he added, "I bet you'll never accept a lift from a stranger again."

DNA analysis positively matched Colin Pitchfork to the semen left behind at both crime scenes. It was the first time DNA was used in a murder conviction.

Pitchfork pleaded guilty to two counts of murder, two counts of rape, two counts of indecent assault, and one count of conspiracy to pervert the course of justice for the false DNA sample.

His guilty plea meant that the prosecution did not need to present the DNA evidence in court, although it had been crucial in identifying him as the perpetrator.

On January 22, 1988, Colin Pitchfork was sentenced to life in prison with a minimum term of thirty years. However, the judge recommended that he should never be released unless it could be proven that he no longer posed a danger to the public.

In 2016, Colin Pitchfork went before the Parole Board to determine his suitability for release. Although he had been a model prisoner and taken part in rehabilitation programs, the families of Lynda Mann and Dawn Ashworth strongly opposed his release, arguing that he still posed a danger to the public.

As a result, his parole was denied. However, Pitchfork was instead transferred to an open prison.

In 2018, Pitchfork appeared before the Parole Board once more, facing opposition from the victims' families who campaigned against his release. Despite his parole being denied, Pitchfork was granted unescorted day trips from prison to assist in his preparation for eventual release.

In June 2021, despite an intense public backlash, the Parole Board granted Pitchfork's release but required him to adhere to strict monitoring.

However, his freedom was short-lived. Pitchfork violated the conditions of his release by approaching two young girls, leading the Parole Board to revoke his release and send him back to prison.

Although his legal team challenged the Board's decision, he was ultimately denied parole again in 2023. Colin Pitchfork will again be eligible for parole again in July 2024 — the month of this book's release.

CHAPTER 7
LOVED IT TO DEATH

Donna Jones was born on a cold Christmas morning in 1975 to her parents, James and Irina Jones. Seventeen months later, her younger brother Derek joined the family.

Growing up in Ottawa, Canada, Donna's personality was shaped by her parents' opposing views on life. Her father was a complex man—caring yet prone to aggressive outbursts. Though never violent, his temper was notorious. James held traditional values, firmly believing that wives should honor their husbands. Despite this, Donna's spirit mirrored her mother's. Her brother Derek fondly described her as lively, generous, bubbly, and a ray of sunshine.

Donna Jones was known among her wide circle of friends for her infectious smile and strong work ethic. Yet, beneath her radiant exterior, Donna struggled with insecurities about her weight and a lazy eye—battles that lingered throughout her life.

Summers for Donna were filled with the joy of playing baseball, while winters saw her gracefully ice skating on Ottawa's frozen canals. Ever eager to learn, Donna dived into various classes, exploring massage therapy, dancing, and kickboxing. She was always enthusiastic about expanding her horizons and embracing new challenges.

After graduating from high school, Donna put herself through Carleton University, where she pursued her passion for human resources by taking courses at Algonquin College. Her dedication and hard work paid off when she secured a position as a civil servant with the Canadian Food Inspection Agency.

Donna lived with her parents until 2005, diligently saving her money to pay off her student debts. At twenty-nine, she proudly purchased her own home in Ottawa's Bayshore area. With a stable career, financial security, and a circle of friends who adored her, Donna seemed to have everything she had hoped for in life. The only thing missing was love.

Though approaching thirty, Donna had barely dated. Weighing 162 pounds, she was self-conscious about her weight, and her shyness grew as the years went by without a partner. She confided in her friends about her fear of being alone and her worry that she might never find someone to share her life with. However, in 2005, everything changed when she met Mark Hutt.

Just before her thirtieth birthday, Donna was introduced to Mark Hutt. Mark played on the same baseball team as she did. Mark was three years older than Donna and had grown up in a broken home.

Mark claimed that when he was five years old, he had inadvertently hastened his parents' divorce. One day, he innocently told his mother, "Daddy's girlfriend makes good muffins," revealing his father's infidelity.

For the remainder of his childhood, Mark divided his time between his mother and father. His mother's new relationship brought more turmoil into his life. He often witnessed his mother being beaten and battered by her new partner. The abuse escalated until, eventually, her partner was arrested after breaking her arm.

Mark claimed that life with his father was no better. His father regularly treated him cruelly, and Mark constantly found himself in trouble. One particularly troubling incident occurred when Mark shoved his stepsister off a dock into an icy lake in the middle of winter.

As a teenager, Mark struggled with learning disabilities and attention-deficit/hyperactivity disorder (ADHD). His behavior often led to trouble, with misdemeanors like throwing rocks through windows resulting in frequent police encounters. Mark attended high school for only a few months before dropping out after discovering alcohol and marijuana.

Lacking job skills, Mark struggled to find employment and ended up working for his father, roofing houses. Despite this, Mark often described his life as one big party, using his addictions to minimize and justify his behaviors.

When Donna and Mark met in the summer of 2005, their relationship histories couldn't have been more different. Donna had just experienced a breakup from a brief relationship, her first attempt at dating in a long time. Before meeting Mark, she had never been in a long-term, serious relationship.

In contrast, Mark had recently ended a tumultuous two-year relationship. His ex-girlfriend described their time together as a "roller coaster," noting Mark's Jekyll-and-Hyde personality. She recalled how he could be charming and friendly one moment only to become rageful and aggressive the next.

Desperate to find love, Donna quickly allowed their relationship to progress. Shortly after they started dating, Mark moved into the house she had just purchased. However, Donna's friends and family immediately noticed unsettling changes in her behavior and demeanor.

Early on, it became evident that Mark had a controlling grip on Donna. Whether she was at work or with friends, he would call her constantly, sometimes every fifteen minutes. Friends often overheard Mark shouting at her, calling her names, and having fits of jealous rage. Whenever they called Donna at home, they would hear the familiar click of a second receiver picking up, knowing that Mark was listening in.

Despite the obvious red flags, Donna held on. Her friends and family, however, noticed her withdrawal as she became increasingly unavailable for social gatherings. Donna constantly made excuses for Mark's behavior, and when the signs of physical abuse began to appear, she made excuses for those as well.

When Donna showed up with bruises, she would dismiss them as nothing, claiming she had run into something. Once, when her brother noticed a hand-shaped mark on her skin, she even blamed it on one of Mark's dogs.

In 2006, Donna and Mark took a trip to Disney World in Florida. Despite fighting throughout the trip, Donna couldn't resist when Mark asked her to marry him. Her decision shocked her worried friends and family, who had witnessed the negative changes in her over the past year.

Donna's friends were desperately concerned about her decision to marry Mark Hutt. They were with her when she finally picked out a wedding dress and called Mark to share the good news. His only concern, however, was whether she had done the laundry or not.

After the engagement, Donna gradually stopped taking care of herself. Her coworkers noticed she no longer did her hair or dressed well for work. It was clear she had given up.

Just one month before the wedding, Donna had scheduled her bachelorette party. Her friends, however, were in no mood to celebrate. Instead, they staged an intervention. Each friend prepared a heartfelt speech, pleading with Donna not to marry a man who was clearly abusing her. They even arranged a safe place for her to stay, hoping she would finally wake up and leave him. Despite their efforts, Donna wouldn't listen. She was determined to go through with the marriage.

Her friends were so distraught that several bridesmaids, including her maid of honor, pulled out of the wedding altogether. Despite all the drama and the clear warnings from those who loved her, Donna Jones married Mark Hutt in September 2007.

After the wedding, Donna withdrew from her friends even further. During a random visit, her brother Derek noticed a new truck in the driveway and soon discovered other new purchases—an ATV, a snowmobile, and a pool table. All were gifts from Donna to Mark.

Derek also noticed several holes in the walls, clearly from fists punching through the drywall. Donna was no longer herself. She seemed dazed, as if medicated, and her once bright, happy smile had become a cold, vacant stare.

Just before their marriage, Mark had filed for bankruptcy, leaving Donna to shoulder the burden of his debts. She covered his vehicle payments and medical bills and began buying him expensive gifts. Within two years, her financial stability had vanished. Despite having a good job and being frugal with her money, Donna was now flat-broke. In 2009, she, too, filed for bankruptcy.

As the months passed, Donna's injuries grew increasingly severe. Her broken wrist, now held together by metal pins, was a glaring testament to her suffering. Despite the obvious severity, Donna dismissed it as clumsiness, claiming she had merely slipped on some rocks.

By the sweltering summer of 2009, Donna had lost sixty pounds and walked with a permanent limp. She regularly wore long-sleeve turtleneck sweaters and heavy makeup to conceal the bruises and cigarette burns that marred her body.

Donna had an excuse for every injury. When she showed up at work with severe burns on her hands, she claimed it was just a cooking mishap. Her split lip seemed to be permanent, never having a chance to heal.

As Donna's home life deteriorated, her work life also began to suffer. Once a stellar employee, her performance had noticeably declined. Mark's angry phone calls frequently disrupted her workday, causing concern among her colleagues and supervisors.

By late November 2009, the situation had reached a critical point. Donna called in sick, citing a cold as the reason for her absence. However, her boss, attuned to the signs of potential domestic abuse, sensed that something more serious was wrong. Acting on his instincts, he contacted the police to report his concerns about Donna's welfare. Sadly, this report went uninvestigated.

Frustrated by the lack of official response and increasingly worried about Donna's safety, her coworkers formulated a plan. They decided to organize an intervention, intending to confront Donna about the suspected abuse when she returned to the office. Sadly, they never got the chance.

On the morning of December 6, 2009, just after 9:00 a.m., Mark Hutt made a frantic call to 911. His voice was filled with panic and urgency as he shouted into the phone that his wife, Donna, was not breathing. During the seven-minute call, Mark told the dispatcher that, when he had checked on Donna just three hours earlier, she was alive and well, and they were discussing their Christmas plans.

As emergency responders approached the modest two-story home at 1087 Barwell Avenue, the first thing that struck them as odd was an open window—highly unusual for the depths of a cold Canadian winter.

When they entered the house, the reason for the open window became immediately apparent. They were hit by a pungent, sickly odor that one officer described as unlike anything he had ever encountered. The unmistakable smell of decomposition directly contradicted Mark's claim that Donna had been alive three hours earlier.

They made their way to the basement, where they found a scene that would haunt them for years. Donna Jones' body lay on a makeshift mattress made up of dirty couch pillows. She was dressed in a T-shirt and soiled pajama bottoms.

Paramedics were horrified by what they saw. More than 40% of Donna's body was covered in third and fourth-degree burns. These weren't fresh injuries; the burns were putrid and weeping with an infection so severe that her clothing stuck to the septic wounds. As one of the medics attempted to assess Donna, they found that her T-shirt had fused to her skin, which peeled away as they tried to examine her.

Donna's face was severely swollen, making it unrecognizable. The swelling was so extreme that the paramedics couldn't open her eyes to examine her pupils. Both of her eyes were bruised black. In addition to the burns, her body was covered with numerous cuts and scrapes. Later, one of the emergency responders would describe Donna's appearance by saying she looked as if she had been "dragged behind a car on a gravel road."

It was immediately clear that any attempts at resuscitation

would have been futile. Rigor mortis had set in hours ago, indicating she had been dead for at least twelve hours.

As investigators processed the scene, they uncovered increasingly disturbing details. Blood stains marred the walls, hallway floor, and stair posts, telling a story of violence that had spread throughout the house. A bathroom door stood out, its splintered frame evidence of having been forcibly smashed open. With each new discovery, it became clear that this place, which should have been a sanctuary, had instead become a chamber of horrors.

Mark Hutt's behavior was erratic as he interacted with the first responders. He cycled through periods of agitation and hysteria, interspersed with moments of eerie calmness. However, one particular detail caught the attention of the emergency personnel: when they delivered the news of his wife's death, Mark's reaction was strikingly out of place. Despite the gravity of the situation, he remained dry-eyed, not shedding a single tear for his deceased spouse.

At the scene, Mark provided an explanation for Donna's injuries. He claimed that twelve days earlier, she had fallen into a fire pit, resulting in severe burns. According to Mark, Donna had refused to seek medical attention at a hospital. Instead, he said he had attempted to treat her injuries himself. He described his "treatment" as giving her Tylenol for pain relief, offering puffs from his asthma inhaler when she struggled to breathe, and administering Benadryl to prevent potential allergic reactions.

Just a few hours later, when Mark was brought in for questioning, his story had already changed.

When the interview began, detectives initially treated Hutt as a grieving spouse. However, his behavior raised suspicions.

Despite sniffling and fake crying, Hutt never produced actual tears. At one point, he pretended to vomit into the trash can, but only spit came out.

Initially, Mark stuck to his story about the fire pit but quickly abandoned it for another narrative. He now claimed that he had been making spaghetti. "She loved my spaghetti," he said. "She loved it to death."

But as he set the water on the stove to boil, Donna broke the news that she was leaving him. In a fit of frustration, he hit the pot of boiling water, accidentally scalding Donna, who was crouched behind him.

Throughout the interview, Hutt portrayed himself as a caring husband who had begged Donna to seek medical help. He claimed she had refused, worried about getting him in trouble. He insisted he had stayed up with her, changing bandages and tending to her needs.

However, detectives had already received preliminary forensic information that contradicted his story.

The most immediately apparent injuries were the extensive burns covering approximately 40% of Donna's body. These were third and fourth-degree burns, primarily on her back, arms, and sides. The burns were in an advanced state of infection, emitting a foul odor and exuding fluids. The pattern of the burns, particularly the unburnt areas shaped like crossed arms, indicated that Donna had been in a protective, crouching position when she had been scalded.

Donna's body bore multiple broken and fractured bones, indicating systematic violence over time. Nine of her ribs were fractured, with the pattern suggesting they were caused by kicking. Seven of these rib fractures showed callous formation, signifying older injuries that had started to heal. The other two fractures were recent.

Her nose was broken, her right wrist was fractured, and she had a broken left finger. Her forearm had an older "night-stick" fracture caused by raising an arm to defend against a blow.

Twenty-nine lead pellets were found embedded about one centimeter deep in Donna's skin. They had been deliberately shot into her feet, legs, shoulders, and arms. Some of these pellets were fired after she had been burned, as they were lodged in her already infected burn wounds. The older pellets had begun to cause lead poisoning.

Both fresh and old trauma injuries were found on her head. Countless cuts, bruises, scabs, and scrapes covered her body, particularly on her head, knees, and legs.

Due to the untreated burns and resulting infection, Donna had gone into septic shock. This led to multiple organ failure, which was determined to be the ultimate cause of death.

Based on the state of decomposition and rigor mortis, doctors estimated that Donna had been dead for approximately twelve hours before the 911 call was made, contradicting Mark Hutt's claim that she had been alive just hours earlier.

The autopsy report noted that many of the injuries, particularly the fresh bruises, broken bones, and some of the pellet wounds, were inflicted after Donna had been scalded. This indicated that the abuse had continued even as she lay dying from her burn injuries.

The pathologist also emphasized that if Donna had received proper medical treatment for her burns, she would have had a nearly 100% chance of survival. Instead, she had endured twelve days of excruciating pain and continued abuse before succumbing to her injuries.

When confronted about other injuries found on Donna's body, Hutt's explanations became increasingly implausible. He suggested Donna was clumsy and prone to accidents. He recalled incidents where she had fallen and broken her wrist or where he had accidentally elbowed her nose in his sleep. When confronted about the pellet gun wounds, Hutt claimed he had accidentally shot her while target practicing.

The trial began on May 8, 2013, and lasted four weeks. Hutt pleaded guilty to a lesser charge of criminal negligence causing death, but the prosecution rejected this plea and pursued a first-degree murder charge.

The prosecution presented a mountain of evidence. They called multiple witnesses, including Donna's pathologist, who detailed the extensive injuries found during the autopsy. A burns expert testified that Donna would have been in "exquisite pain," but she would have had a nearly 100% chance of survival if given proper medical treatment.

Hutt's defense team didn't deny the abuse or the scalding. Instead, they argued that the prosecution hadn't proven Hutt's intention was for Donna to die. They suggested that if Hutt had wanted to kill Donna, he would have had ample ways to do so and dispose of the evidence. No witnesses were called for the defense.

The jury needed less than a day to reach their verdict. On June 7, 2013, they found Mark Hutt guilty of first-degree murder. In Canada, this conviction comes with an automatic life sentence with no possibility of parole for twenty-five years.

CHAPTER 8
THE FRENCH NANNY

In the 1980s, Algeria, situated on the northern coast of Africa along the Mediterranean Sea, faced economic challenges, including high unemployment, inflation, and shortages of essential goods. The government enforced tight control, restricting political freedom and suppressing dissent. As a result, widespread social unrest, protests, and strikes occurred, notably culminating in the violent October 1988 riots fueled by economic grievances. The government's harsh crackdown on these protests led to numerous casualties and increased tensions significantly.

By the late 1980s, Algeria was teetering on the brink of civil war, prompting many Algerians to seek improved economic prospects abroad, particularly in France.

Born in 1982, Sabrina Kouider was still a young girl when her family fled Algeria for a better life in Paris. However, in her early teens, Sabrina began displaying concerning behavior. After injuring her back, she was prescribed strong painkillers, which eventually led to addiction. By her mid-teens, she had overdosed twice.

During her teenage years, those who knew her described Sabrina as bossy, narcissistic, and volatile, often erupting in anger toward her classmates. She was known for seeking attention and struggled to maintain friendships, especially with other girls whom she perceived as rivals.

From an early age, Sabrina Kouider was fixated on celebrities and the glamorous lifestyles they led. She harbored a strong, desperate desire to achieve fame herself despite lacking any skills or talents that could realistically propel her to such celebrity status.

Despite her ambitions, in 2000, at the age of eighteen, Sabrina took a job selling crepes at a carnival, where she met twenty-four-year-old Ouissem "Sam" Medouni. Sabrina—with her long, silky black hair, dark eyes, and smooth olive skin—attracted attention wherever she went. Sam was immediately captivated by Sabrina's stunning appearance, and the two began a romantic relationship.

At the time, Sam was studying for a master's degree in economics. When he completed his studies, he started working at Société Générale, one of France's prominent banks.

Throughout the following years, Sam and Sabrina's relationship was constantly in flux. It was clear that she was the dominant figure in the relationship. While Sabrina liked to draw attention to herself, Sam was happy in the background. He funded her extravagant lifestyle with his well-paid jobs, and she repaid him by sleeping with other men. However, each time, when she'd had enough of other men, Sam would always welcome her back with open arms. Despite being controlling, manipulative, and physically abusive to him, he was always there to pick up the pieces. His friend saw him as weak and easily led, but he would be forever powerless to her.

In 2009, during one of the numerous breaks in their relationship, Sabrina vanished from Sam's life. Without any warning, she left Paris and relocated to London. Feeling that her life was stagnant in Paris, she believed she could either become a celebrity or at least a fashion designer for celebrities in London. However, lacking any experience in the fashion industry, Sabrina ended up taking a job at a NatWest Bank branch in Notting Hill.

When Sam inevitably realized she had moved to London, she asked him not to follow, but Sam couldn't stand the idea of being without her. He moved to London too and got a job with a French bank. Despite the continued volatility in their relationship, Sabrina gave birth to her first son in 2010.

In the early 1990s, Mark Walton and his friend Shane Lynch helped create the Irish boy band Boyzone. Although his time with the band was short-lived, Walton went on to establish himself as a powerhouse in the music industry, working with artists such as Jennifer Lopez and Lady Gaga, eventually becoming a multi-billionaire.

In 2011, when Mark Walton walked into the Notting Hill branch of NatWest Bank and saw Sabrina Kouider's big brown eyes and soft French accent, he described it as "love at first sight." Walton introduced himself, but Sabrina, already immersed in her celebrity obsession, was already familiar with who he was.

After their initial meeting, Mark Walton and Sabrina spoke daily and quickly fell in love. Sabrina felt she had found her ideal partner—if she couldn't achieve celebrity status herself, dating Mark Walton was the next best thing. Within months, they moved in together, and Sabrina became an instant London socialite.

As their relationship progressed, Sabrina told Mark stories of abuse during her childhood in an attempt to gain his pity. Later, he would realize that none of it was true. She just needed him to focus all of his attention on her.

Sabrina's insatiable need for Mark Walton's undivided attention quickly strained their relationship. As a celebrity and music executive, Walton's frequent interactions with other women sparked intense jealousy and led to abusive behavior from Sabrina. She would publicly berate him and once even physically assaulted a woman she deemed more attractive than herself.

While shopping at high-end shops on Oxford Street in London, she once screamed, "Mr. Boyzone has no money!" and stormed out of the store like an angry child when he refused to purchase something she desired.

Walton later recalled that Sabrina would punch him in the jaw if he snored too loudly. On another occasion, she threatened to beat him with an ashtray when he questioned her about pictures of her with another man.

After fourteen months of physical and mental abuse, Walton ended the relationship and moved to Los Angeles, calling his time with Sabrina the most turbulent relationship he'd ever had. He had hoped to put Sabrina Kouider behind him, but he had no way of knowing she wasn't done with him.

Shortly after Mark Walton arrived in Los Angeles in 2012, he received news that Sabrina was pregnant. However, uncertainty lingered over whether he was the father. Worried about the situation, he asked for a paternity test, but Sabrina refused.

Despite the uncertainty, Mark assumed he was the father and started sending her money every month. He persisted in asking for a paternity test, but Sabrina consistently refused. By early 2014, after several months of sending payments, Mark stopped the financial support and ended all communication with Sabrina.

After Mark Walton left for Los Angeles, Sabrina Kouider's life rapidly spiraled downward. Losing her connection to celebrity circles and the lavish lifestyle she had become accustomed to left her in turmoil. Desperate, she sought solace in the one person who had consistently forgiven her abusive behavior: Sam Medouni.

Sam, always willing to forgive, welcomed Sabrina back into his life. Years earlier, unable to resist her allure, he had followed her to London, and now, once more, he embraced her. The couple settled into a £1 million rented house in the Wimbledon suburb, a sharp contrast to the life Sabrina believed she deserved.

As they settled into their new life together, Sabrina's mental state began to deteriorate rapidly. The loss of Mark and the lifestyle he had provided gnawed at her, fueling a growing paranoia and obsession. Unable to accept that Mark had left her, Sabrina constructed an elaborate fantasy in which he was stalking her, unable to let her go.

This delusion took a sinister turn as Sabrina began to file police reports against Mark. Between 2014 and 2016, she made more than thirty false accusations, each more outlandish than the last. She claimed Mark was stalking her, hacking into her phones and email. She accused him of sending helicopters to fly over her home—a claim that baffled authorities, considering that Mark lived 5,400 miles away in Los Angeles.

The accusations didn't end there. One of the most bizarre claims was that Mark Walton had sexually abused her cat—a pet she didn't even own. Her fabrications were limitless; she accused him of harming her family and even of using black magic to manipulate her.

The police, initially taking her claims seriously, soon began to see through the web of lies. In July 2014, they questioned Mark based on Sabrina's allegations of harassment, only to release him without charge when they found no evidence to support her claims. Eventually, the authorities had had enough of Sabrina's false reports and cautioned her against making more baseless accusations.

But the warning fell on deaf ears. Sabrina's obsession with Mark only intensified. She created fake Facebook profiles to spread her lies, accusing him of being violent, an animal abuser, and even a child abuser. She sent these slanderous posts to Mark's close social circle and family members, intent on destroying his reputation.

As Sabrina's delusions spiraled out of control, Sam found himself drawn deeper into her twisted world. Despite his initial skepticism, he began to adopt her paranoid beliefs, becoming a willing participant in her fantasies. The couple's shared delusion would soon create a dangerous environment for anyone who entered their orbit.

In the summer of 2016, Sabrina Kouider and Sam Medouni found themselves in a precarious financial situation. Despite living in a rented £1 million home in the upscale suburb of Wimbledon, their bank accounts told a different story. Sam's once lucrative career as a financial analyst had taken a downturn, and Sabrina's attempts at breaking into the fashion industry had yielded nothing but mounting debt.

The couple frequently fell behind on their rent, occasionally missing payments altogether. Their neighbors started to notice their unpredictable behavior, including Sabrina leaving garbage outside their front door, which attracted local foxes and contributed to the overall neglect of their once-well-kept home.

Yet, despite their dire financial straits, Sabrina couldn't shake the feeling that her life raising two children was too difficult to manage on her own. The idea of hiring an au pair began to take root in her mind. She envisioned someone who could take care of the household chores, look after the children, and allow her to focus on her elusive dreams of fame and fortune.

Their decision to hire an au pair flew in the face of all financial logic. They could barely afford their rent, let alone the additional expense of an employee. But Sabrina, never one to let reality interfere with her desires, pressed forward with the plan.

The couple posted an advertisement, offering a paltry £50 per week—far below the standard rate for au pairs in London. Still, the advertisement caught the eye of Sophie Lionnet, a twenty-year-old from a small French town who was eager for adventure and a chance to improve her English. Sophie, in her youthful naivety, saw only the opportunity for experience in a foreign country, unaware of the financial instability and mounting delusions that plagued her future employers.

When Sophie Lionnet arrived in London in January 2016, the initial atmosphere at the household seemed promising. She was greeted by what appeared to be a picture-perfect young family living in an upscale neighborhood.

Sabrina, with her glamorous appearance and claims of celebrity connections, must have seemed exciting to the shy young woman from a small French town. Sam Medouni initially presented a kinder, more stable counterpart to Sabrina's flamboyant personality. For Sophie, who loved music and ice skating and had a natural affinity for childcare, it seemed like an ideal opportunity to improve her English and gain valuable experience.

Sophie was a kind, quiet, and shy young woman. She had studied childcare and early years education at college but couldn't find work in her small French town. Despite the trivial wage, she was thrilled to move to London, gain work experience, and learn English.

Sophie threw herself into her new job with enthusiasm. She cared for the couple's two children, and her gentle nature made her a natural with the kids. She explored the local area, visited nearby shops and cafes, and slowly became a familiar face in the neighborhood.

Sophie had a heavy workload from the start. Yet, in her eagerness to please and make the most of her opportunity, she didn't complain. Neighbors and local shopkeepers noticed Sophie's quiet, reserved demeanor, and she quickly became well-liked in the neighborhood. However, she maintained a distance from others outside of the home.

As the weeks went by, the initially positive atmosphere began to sour. Sabrina's attitude toward Sophie gradually turned more demanding and critical. Sophie's workload grew heavier, now including cleaning the entire house in addition to her childcare responsibilities. Her working hours extended to over seventy-five hours per week, all for the same meager pay.

Despite these challenges, Sophie remained dedicated to her job. She lacked the confidence to express her concerns or seek assistance. Her limited English skills and separation from her family and friends left her susceptible to the growing control exerted by her employers.

Sophie communicated with her parents in France via Facebook whenever she could, but by the summer of 2017, Sabrina's treatment of Sophie had grown increasingly erratic and abusive. Sophie confided in her parents, expressing that she was experiencing verbal abuse and wanted to return home.

It started with small, seemingly innocuous comments. Sabrina criticized Sophie's cleaning, claiming corners were missed or tasks were left unfinished. Her voice, once warm and encouraging, now took on a sharp, biting edge, often calling her "useless" or "stupid" for not understanding instructions in English.

Then accusations of theft followed, with Sabrina accusing Sophie of stealing her diamond necklace. She would confront Sophie in the kitchen or living room, launching into prolonged, angry tirades about these perceived injustices. Sophie, timid and eager to appease, stood silently, nodding and murmuring agreement, uncertain how to respond to the increasingly aggressive outbursts.

As Sabrina became more entrenched in her delusions about Mark Walton, her verbal abuse turned increasingly ominous. She started questioning Sophie's loyalty, accusing her of deceit and concealment. "What are you hiding from me?" she would demand, her voice dropping to a menacing tone. "I know you're hiding something. You can't fool me."

These interrogations, initially sporadic, became more frequent and intense. Sabrina would corner Sophie late at night, bombarding her with questions about Mark Walton, a man Sophie had never met. "I know you're working for him," Sabrina would insist, her voice rising to a shout. "Stop lying to me!"

Sophie, confused and frightened, would try to deny these accusations, but her protests only seemed to fuel Sabrina's anger. "You're a liar!" Sabrina would scream, her face inches from Sophie's. "A dirty, lying spy!"

In late August, Sabrina dragged a visibly frightened Sophie to the local police station, demanding that she confess to a non-existing relationship with Mark Walton. She also accused Sophie of plotting to kill Sabrina's family. The police, unaware of the abuse Sophie was going through at home yet recognizing that Sabrina was delusional, let them go after an awkward conversation.

Sabrina was becoming increasingly neurotic, and Sam Medouni supported every move Sabrina made. In addition to withholding Sophie's pay, she was restricting her food and had taken her passport to ensure she couldn't return home. Neighbors and shop owners in the area noticed that by that fall, Sophie's once healthy frame had become skeletal, her cheeks hollow, and her eyes sunken. When she walked into the corner shop, the shopkeeper often saw tears in her eyes.

On September 20, 2017, a neighbor dialed 999 when they saw billowing black smoke pouring over the fence of Sam Medouni's Wimbledon Park Road address. A large bonfire was burning in the backyard that seemed too close to a wooden patio. More unsettling, however, was the putrid smell of the fire.

When firefighters arrived, Sam Medouni was grilling several pieces of chicken on a barbeque grill situated near the roaring bonfire. When asked why the bonfire smelled so bad, Sam was quick to blame it on the chicken. However, when firefighters saw bones in the bonfire, Sam calmly claimed there was nothing to worry about—it was only a lamb carcass. He insisted he was a sheep farmer, even though he lived in suburban London.

Despite his explanation, the bonfire was illegal in the area, and firefighters swiftly extinguished it. Once the flames were quelled, it became evident that it wasn't a lamb carcass burning at all. Among the smoldering ashes, they discovered fingers, fragments of a human nose, and melted women's jewelry and glasses.

Sam Medouni and Sabrina Kouider were both taken into custody on suspicion of murder and questioned at separate police stations. The couple quickly turned on each other. Both denied any involvement in the murder of Sophie Lionnet and claimed the other one had murdered her. Forensic examination, however, would reveal the true story of Sophie's death.

In the last two weeks of Sophie's life, Sabrina and Sam had recorded dozens of hours of audio of their relentless torture. They spent hours trying to get Sophie to admit that she was sleeping with and secretly spying for Mark Walton. They repeatedly slapped, punched, and beat her with an electrical cord, eventually breaking five of her ribs, fracturing her mandible, and breaking her sternum.

One photo taken with Sabrina's phone showed an emaciated and exhausted Sophie after going days or even weeks with very little food.

The couple had taken away her money, passport, wallet, and a plane ticket home that her mother had purchased for her. In the weeks leading up to her death, they kept her locked in a small, dark room, only allowing her out to use the bathroom.

The couple relentlessly screamed at her to confess something she hadn't done. In addition to the accusations of an affair with Walton and spying for him, they accused her of abusing their children and stealing jewelry from the house.

In the grip of her delusional paranoia, Sabrina Kouider concocted a horrifying scenario. She accused the young nanny of secretly drugging Sam, rendering him defenseless. According to Sabrina's warped logic, this incapacitation was meant to allow Mark Walton's entry into their home, where he would then sexually violate the unconscious Sam.

Although the accusation was ridiculous and completely unfounded, Sophie was already weakened by days of physical abuse, food deprivation, and psychological torment. She found herself at her breaking point. In a desperate attempt to end her suffering, she succumbed to their demands. Believing that an admission might finally bring her ordeal to an end, Sophie falsely confessed to spying for Mark Walton.

However, Sophie's hopes for relief were cruelly dashed. Rather than providing the reprieve she desperately sought, her confession seemed to fuel her tormentors' frenzy. In a horrifying escalation, Sabrina and Sam forcibly moved Sophie to the bathroom. There, in a scene of unimaginable cruelty, they subjected her to waterboarding in the bathtub. This brutal act, with water running over her face as she struggled for air, ultimately led to Sophie's tragic drowning.

Later that day, without a shred of remorse, the couple had sex just a few feet away from Sophie's lifeless body.

A psychological evaluation of the couple after their arrest revealed that Sabrina suffered from borderline personality disorder and depression, yet neither diagnosis would get her out of her responsibility for the crime.

At trial, the prosecution painted a horrific picture of paranoia, abuse, and murder. More than eight hours of audio recording were played for the jury, showing the merciless torment Sophie Lionnet was forced to endure before her death.

Sabrina Kouider's face was contorted in anger as Mark Walton took the stand to testify about the absurd delusions he had encountered during their time together.

Both Sam and Sabrina stuck to their stories of blaming the other. They contradicted each other at every turn, painting themselves as victims in the whole ordeal, but the jury took note of their obvious lack of remorse for what they had done to the innocent girl.

On May 24, 2018, after thirty hours of deliberation, the jury returned a guilty verdict on all counts. Sabrina Kouider screamed and collapsed in tears, while Sam Medouni simply hung his head in shame.

A month later, at sentencing, Sabrina read a prepared letter of apology to Sophie, but the words were too little too late. Ouissem "Sam" Medouni and Sabrina Kouider were each sentenced to life in prison with a minimum term of thirty years.

CHAPTER 9
LUMINOL AND LIES

In 1969, at the age of twenty-five, Bill Mowbray became the youngest Cadillac dealer in the United States. Bill's father and grandfather had both worked in the automotive industry and Bill was determined to make his mark.

By 1974, his dealership in Brownsville, Texas—Bill Mowbray Motors—had flourished, employing forty-five people and spanning five acres. The dealership offered a diverse selection of new and used vehicles from Cadillac, Oldsmobile, Pontiac, and Mazda.

Despite Bill Mowbray's business success, he felt unfulfilled. In the late 1970s, he began cheating on his wife. When she discovered his infidelity and threatened to leave, Bill attempted suicide. Though he survived, their marriage did not.

Shortly after his divorce, Bill met and married Susie Burnett, a sweet woman with sun-kissed blonde hair and a gentle voice. Bill shared custody of his daughter, Kristin, from his first marriage, while Susie had two children, Wade and

Cricket, from hers. Together, they formed a big, happy family.

Over the years, Bill Mowbray Motors continued to grow and thrive, making Bill one of the wealthiest men in Brownsville. Bill and Susie became well-known figures in the community, frequently appearing in the dealership's commercials that aired throughout South Texas.

The substantial income from the dealership fed Bill's lavish lifestyle. Known for his extravagant tastes, Bill loved to spend money. He built a massive home on a large lakeside property and owned two condos on the beach.

Despite his apparent financial success, Bill was spending money faster than he was making it. By the mid-1980s, he had taken out two loans against his car lots, each using the same property as collateral. Overwhelmed by debt, Bill found himself in a dire financial situation with no clear way out. To make matters worse, he owed several hundred thousand dollars to the IRS.

Bill hadn't learned his lesson from his first marriage and was seeing another woman. When Susie discovered his infidelity, she took her two children and moved to Austin for nine months. Desperate, Bill pleaded for her return, claiming he couldn't live without her and threatening to kill himself if she didn't come back.

Susie and the children returned to Brownsville and moved back in with Bill, but rumors circulated that she had only come back for the money and that their relationship was effectively over. For all intents and purposes, their marriage had run its course.

After Susie returned, she and Bill visited his lawyer. The lawyer informed Susie that since Bill had purchased the house before their relationship began, he had the legal right to evict her if she filed for divorce. He explained that Bill could obtain a restraining order to force her out, leaving her with no claim to the property or its contents.

In mid-September 1987, Bill was at his breaking point, convinced that an indictment for defrauding the IRS was imminent. Desperate for money, he approached every bank he had a relationship with, seeking loans. However, he had already borrowed too much, and no bank was willing to lend him the amount he needed to escape the financial hole he had dug for himself.

Knowing that the dealership was destined to go under, Luke Fruia, Bill's good friend and right-hand man at the car dealership, let Bill know he was planning to leave his position. With his world collapsing around him, Bill confided in Luke, declaring that he would rather kill himself than go to jail.

Luke was familiar with Bill's suicidal threats. Bill's history of depression was common knowledge, and Luke was aware of Bill's two previous suicide attempts.

On the evening of September 16, 1987, Bill and Susie retired for the night. Bill took medication for his chronic back pain, while Susie stayed up to read. To block the light from disturbing him, Bill placed a mound of pillows between them. About an hour later, Susie turned off the light and went to sleep.

Late that night, Susie awoke to the sound of sobbing on Bill's side of the bed. When she opened her eyes, in the dark, she could barely see his elbow pointed in the air with his hand near his head. When she reached over to touch his elbow, however, she was shocked to hear a deafening gunshot. Susie jumped out of bed and rushed to Bill's side of the bed. Unable to see in the dark, she reached for his face, but felt only wet, mangled flesh and blood. She touched the bed next to him and picked up a .357 Magnum revolver that had fallen in a pool of his blood. Susie screamed, dropped the gun, and ran downstairs to the telephone.

Susie first called Luke Fruia, a close friend of both her and Bill. In a hysterical panic, she screamed, "He did it. He really did it! He actually killed himself!" Luke urged her to call 911 immediately and assured her that he would be right there.

Frantic, Susie called 911 and reported that her husband had committed suicide in their bed. When police arrived, they found a distressed Susie Mowbray outside the front door, clutching a cocktail glass in one hand and a cigarette in the other. When officers asked what had happened, she pointed to the second floor of the house and said, "He's up there."

Emergency responders found thirty-nine-year-old Bill Mowbray still gurgling for breath but quickly circling the drain. Sadly, by the time they got him to the hospital, he had died.

Bill had been lying on his left side when the bullet entered his right temple. The powerful gun had left a massive wound on the right side of his head. Blood soaked the sheets, mattress, floor, headboard, and bedside table. Blood had spattered onto the wall above the bed, while more blood spatters peppered the ceiling and the ceiling fan above.

Bill's left hand, which was tucked beneath his head, had a bullet hole through the palm after it exited the left side of his skull. His right hand was near his chest beneath the sheets.

When police spoke to Susie, she explained that she had always known Bill would do it someday and had expected it. Others who knew him corroborated her story, acknowledging that Bill's emotional and mental issues were well-known, though no one believed he would actually follow through.

One of the officers who first responded to the scene was Lieutenant George Gavito of the Cameron County Sheriff's Department. Gavito had known Bill, and he, too, had known of Bill's suicidal tendencies. To Gavito, the case seemed obvious: it was indeed suicide. That evening, the police gave their condolences to the family and said they would return the next day to follow up with them.

In the early afternoon the following day, Bill's daughter Kristin returned to the house with her uncle, Bill's brother. As they entered, they were surprised to hear female voices and music coming from upstairs. When they entered the master bedroom, they discovered Susie and two friends painting the blood-stained walls. When Kristin asked what was going on, Susie casually replied that they were having a painting party.

Bill's brother was furious and called the police to report that the crime scene had not been secured and evidence had not been preserved. However, the previous night, the police had concluded that Bill's death was a suicide and had not sealed the room as a crime scene. Susie explained that they were cleaning up and painting over the stains to prevent her children from seeing the blood and brain matter in the house.

Susie Mowbray's decision to clean up the crime scene prompted investigators to re-examine Bill's death. They collected the sheets, mattress, pillows, and Susie's nightgown from the home and brought them in for analysis.

In the days after Bill's death, an autopsy revealed crucial details that put a gaping hole in the suicide theory. No gunshot residue or high-impact blood spatter was found on Bill's right hand or forearm. His left hand was beneath his head with a gunshot through it, so it was clear he hadn't used his left hand to shoot the gun. With that information, the medical examiner determined that suicide was an impossibility, and the death was ruled a homicide.

Investigators also discovered that Susie Mowbray had recently inquired about Bill's life insurance policy, valued at nearly $1.8 million dollars. In the days leading up to his death, Bill had decided to change the beneficiary to his daughter but never completed the paperwork. Investigators learned that Susie was aware of his intention. However, since Bill died before making the change, Susie remained the sole beneficiary.

Seven weeks after Bill's death, on November 3, the forensic analysis of Susie's nightgown was completed. Investigators had enlisted Dusty Hesskew, a blood spatter expert from the Austin Police Department, to examine the garment. Hesskew performed a luminol test and discovered high-impact blood spatter, indicating that Susie had shot Bill at close range. He concluded that Susie had held the gun eighteen to twenty-four inches above Bill's head and shot him in the right temple.

Based on Hesskew's findings, Susie Mowbray was arrested on suspicion of murdering her husband.

Six months later, Susie Mowbray went on trial for murder. The prosecution's case largely revolved around Dusty Hesskew's blood spatter testimony. The nightgown was presented to the jury, and although no blood was visible to the naked eye, Hesskew assured the court that he had confirmed its presence during the brief period it was highlighted by the luminol test.

Hesskew testified that the only way the blood could have gotten on the nightgown was if Susie had been standing above Bill when she had shot him.

After a four-week trial, the jury returned with a verdict after only a few minutes of deliberation. Susie Mowbray was found guilty of murder and sentenced to life in prison without the possibility of parole.

Susie maintained her innocence, insisting that Bill had committed suicide, but her claims fell on deaf ears as she began serving her sentence. In the years following her conviction, Susie's family, particularly her son Wade Burnett, never gave up hope of proving her innocence. Wade, who was only sixteen at the time of his mother's arrest, took it upon himself to investigate the case and prove his mother's innocence.

As he delved deeper into the case files and court documents, Wade discovered several discrepancies and inconsistencies in the evidence used to convict his mother. One of the most significant pieces of evidence was the testimony of Dusty

Hesskew, the blood spatter expert who claimed to have found blood on Susie's nightgown.

Wade diligently sifted through court records and the mountains of paperwork involved with the case. Meanwhile, Susie repeatedly appealed her conviction, but each time, she was denied.

After nearly a decade behind bars, Wade finally discovered something that he believed could overturn his mother's conviction. He found significant issues with Dusty Hesskew's blood spatter analysis of Susie's nightgown. Additionally, he uncovered that the prosecution had hired a second blood-spatter expert who had concluded there was no evidence of blood on the nightgown at all. However, the second expert's findings were never disclosed to the defense and were not presented at trial.

Dusty Hesskew reported that his luminol test on the nightgown had revealed tiny specks of blood. However, luminol tests are presumptive and can react to substances other than blood, such as bleach, copper, and certain root vegetables like horseradish. Therefore, a positive luminol test does not conclusively prove the presence of blood.

Hesskew hadn't performed any tests to confirm that the spots he had observed were indeed blood. Furthermore, he hadn't documented his analysis. Since the specks weren't visible to the naked eye, verifying his results was impossible.

Wade also discovered the analysis done by renowned blood spatter expert Herbert MacDonnell, who had also worked on the O.J. Simpson trial. MacDonnell found no visible blood stains or high-velocity impact spatter on the nightgown. His analysis had been based on established protocols, contrasting sharply with Hesskew's questionable and unverified methods.

After more than nine years, Wade Burnett's hard work finally paid off. During an appeal hearing in 1997, Dusty Hesskew testified that his original blood spatter findings were scientifically invalid. Consequently, the Court of Appeals granted Susie Mowbray a new trial.

Susie's new trial began in January 1998. The defense focused on discrediting Dusty Hesskew's original testimony and highlighting Bill's severe depression, suicidal tendencies, and financial problems. They called Hesskew as a hostile witness, and under questioning, he again admitted that his original findings were scientifically flawed.

The defense also emphasized that the prosecution had withheld Herbert MacDonnell's exculpatory evidence during the first trial. They pointed out that blood had splattered all over the room, including the mattress, sheets, ceiling, and the wall behind Bill, yet Susie had been wearing a white nightgown with no visible blood spatter.

The defense also called witnesses who testified about Bill Mowbray's history of depression, suicidal tendencies, and financial troubles. One witness, Dial Dunkin, president of a local bank, recounted a distressing encounter with Bill just days before his death. Bill had entered the bank nearly in tears, desperately begging for a loan of several hundred thousand dollars. Without collateral to support such a large loan, Dunkin had been forced to refuse. Bill, visibly distressed, had laid his head on Dunkin's desk and sobbed, "If you can't help me, I'm just going to have to kill myself.

There's no way I'm going to go to jail." Dunkin described how Bill had been shaking with fear, repeatedly expressing his intent to kill himself before finally leaving the bank in tears.

One of Bill Mowbray's lawyers also testified that, in the days before his death, Bill had asked her to review his life insurance policies to see if they had a suicide clause that may render them invalid if he were to commit suicide.

The defense argued that the police had mishandled the crime scene and failed to properly investigate alternative explanations for Bill's death. They highlighted that the police had initially treated the case as a suicide, allowing Susie and her friends to clean up the scene before conducting a thorough investigation.

The prosecution, however, had purged all the physical evidence against Susie Mowbray, including the nightgown, which had been discarded after more than ten years. This time, they changed their approach, claiming that Susie must have hidden behind the barrier of pillows on the bed when she killed her husband. They argued that this theory explained the lack of blood on her nightgown.

The prosecution argued that, although Bill did have IRS problems, there was no evidence suggesting he would be arrested or indicted for tax fraud. They also highlighted that when first responders arrived at the scene, Bill Mowbray was still alive. However, Susie was outside with a drink in her hand and had made no attempt to help her husband.

During closing arguments, Susie's emotions took over, and she yelled, "I didn't do this! I'm innocent!" before putting her head down on the desk in front of her and crying. To spectators in the courtroom, however, the outburst seemed rehearsed. She was temporarily removed from the courtroom for several minutes before proceedings continued.

On January 21, 1998, after ten hours of deliberation, the jury informed the judge they couldn't reach a unanimous decision. The judge sent them back to deliberate further, instructing them not to return until they had reached a verdict.

After two days of intense deliberation, the jury finally returned with a verdict: not guilty. Susie Mowbray was acquitted of all charges. However, in an unusual move, the jury foreman handed the judge a note. The note read:

> "Members of the jury have reached a conclusion that the only issue decided by this jury is that the prosecution was unable to prove, beyond a reasonable doubt, the guilt of the defendant."

In essence, the jury was avoiding making a definitive claim about Susie Mowbray's innocence or guilt. Instead, they emphasized that their only responsibility was to decide whether the prosecution had proven she had killed him. In their view, the prosecution had failed to make that case.

This case left those in South Texas with more questions than answers. To this day, there are those who profess Susie Mowbray's innocence, as well as those who insist she got away with murder.

After Susie Mowbray's acquittal, she filed lawsuits against Cameron County, the three prosecutors, three police officers including Dusty Hesskew, a Cameron County lab technician, and Bill's daughter and relatives.

In her lawsuit, Susie alleged various claims, such as conspiracy to violate her civil rights, false imprisonment, malicious prosecution, abuse of process, slander, and intentional infliction of emotional distress.

Additionally, she sought to regain the proceeds from Bill's life insurance policy. Following her conviction in the first trial, the life insurance money, amounting to approximately $1.8 million, had been awarded to Bill's daughter, Kristin, and his ex-wife, Virginia Hale. Ultimately, Susie Mowbray lost all of the lawsuits.

CHAPTER 10
THE SLUMBER PARTY

Sandi Folden and Fernando Nieves met as teenagers in the late 1970s, both just fifteen years old. Their bond at Buena Park High School was instant and intense—they were inseparable, sharing every possible moment together. By graduation, their love story had already set its course. In 1983, at the tender age of nineteen, they sealed their commitment with a wedding, and Sandi Folden became Sandi Nieves, ready to embark on a new chapter with her high school sweetheart.

In quick succession, Fernando and Sandi welcomed three children: David, Nikolet, and Rashel. However, their young marriage unraveled, leading to a divorce within three years. Sandi was awarded custody of the children. Fernando remarried swiftly, and his new wife formed a good relationship with the kids. Remarkably, both families managed to maintain a friendly dynamic, coming together for holidays, birthdays, and other celebrations, putting the well-being of the children first.

Sandi's mother, Delores, faced her own marital issues and divorced Sandi's stepfather, David Folden, in 1987. In an unexpected turn of events, Sandi grew closer to her former stepfather, and just two years later, she and David Folden were married.

Sandi and David's relationship began smoothly. David adopted Sandi's three children from her first marriage to Fernando, and together, they had two more children, Kristl and Jaqlene. Despite their efforts, the marriage was far from perfect. After eight years, the couple separated in February 1997.

Unlike her amicable divorce from Fernando, Sandi's separation from David was contentious. The divorce proceedings were marred by a bitter battle over their biological children, Kristl and Jaqlene.

Sandi accused David's adult son from a previous relationship of drug problems and violent behavior that endangered her children. She obtained a restraining order against him, but according to Sandi, he regularly violated it. On the other hand, David alleged that Sandi was physically abusing their children, claiming she beat them with a long wooden spoon.

Financial issues further strained the marriage. Sandi, a stay-at-home mom, was unemployed and couldn't afford to raise five children on her own. David, meanwhile, refused to pay child support for the three children he had adopted. In the spring of 1998, he filed to revoke his adoption of David, Nikolet, and Rashel. Sandi knew that even if she secured custody of Kristl and Jaqlene, she wouldn't be able to provide for them without financial support.

Shortly after separating from David, Sandi met Scott Folk. Their brief and tumultuous relationship lasted only two months. In mid-June, Sandi discovered she was pregnant with Scott's child. When she shared the news, Scott made it clear he had no desire for children. Devastated by his rejection and the prospect of raising another child alone, Sandi made the difficult decision to have an abortion on June 27.

As June drew to a close, Fernando and his wife welcomed all five children to their home to celebrate David's fourteenth birthday. During the festivities, Sandi discussed the ongoing custody battle she was facing. She showed Fernando her will and insurance policies, expressing that if anything happened to her, she wanted him to have custody of all five children.

Later, as Fernando returned the children to Sandi's home in Santa Clarita, California, an uneasy feeling settled over him. He couldn't shake the sense that something was wrong, noting a shift in Sandi's demeanor that left him deeply unsettled.

On the evening of June 30, Sandi Nieves proposed an unusual treat for her children. She suggested a slumber party on the kitchen floor—an idea that delighted her four daughters. Excited, the girls hurried to fetch their sleeping bags.

David, at fourteen, considered himself too mature for such childish activities. He declined to join his sisters, opting instead to sleep in his bedroom as usual.

As the girls settled onto the kitchen floor, none of them could have known the significance of this seemingly innocent family moment.

In the early afternoon of July 1, 1998, Sandy Nieves called 911 to report that there had been a fire in her house. Her voice was slow and slurred as if she were drugged or intoxicated.

Dispatch: 911

Sandi: Hello?

Dispatch: What is your emergency?

Sandi: The house is all smoke.

Dispatch: It's smoking?

Sandi: No, not now. It's over.

Dispatch: Okay.

Sandi: We had a fire last night. I woke up, and everything was black.

Dispatch: Okay, you had a fire there last night?

Sandi: Uh-huh.

Dispatch: You just woke up?

Sandi: Right.

Dispatch: You were sleeping the whole time during the fire?

Sandi: Yeah, I assume.

Dispatch: Where are the kids at right now?

Sandi: Um, on the floor.

Dispatch: On the floor—what?

Sandi: In the kitchen.

Dispatch: Sleeping? Are they injured?

Sandi: I don't know. I don't know what condition they're in.

The 911 operator's confusion added another layer of suspicion to the already perplexing situation. How could someone sleep through a house fire only to report it hours later? This crucial detail immediately raised alarm bells.

Upon entering, they found Sandi and David sitting on the couch, seemingly oblivious to the gravity of the situation. They were casually watching television and eating cookies, but their soot-covered appearances told a different story.

Paramedics sensed that something was not right with the situation and walked further into the house. Sandi, however, insisted everything was fine now, and they could leave. However, as they got further into the home, they were met with the lingering smell of smoke and signs of burn damage.

The walls and floors of the hallway were charred, and more alarmingly, distinct pour patterns on the carpet indicated that someone had deliberately spread flammable liquid.

Upon entering the kitchen, paramedics encountered a scene of unimaginable tragedy. In the center of the room lay four young girls, huddled together in sleeping bags, motionless.

Twelve-year-old Nikolet, eleven-year-old Rashel, seven-year-old Kristl, and five-year-old Jaqlene had succumbed to smoke inhalation. The innocent slumber party had turned into a horrific tragedy.

As investigators arrived and surveyed the kitchen, they quickly uncovered evidence pointing to a deliberate act. The open oven door with its gas turned on and towels stuffed inside painted a chilling picture of premeditation. Another towel on the lit stove burner further confirmed their suspicions.

The investigation continued to uncover damning evidence. The smoke detector, meant to save lives, had been deliberately disabled and lay melted on the floor—a clear attempt to prevent any early detection of the fire.

Traces of gasoline throughout the house, including all three bedrooms, confirmed the fire's intentional nature. The discovery of a large red gasoline can in Sandi's bedroom was particularly incriminating, directly linking her to the arson.

Fire investigators determined that the fire at the Nieves household was intentional, noting the closed windows during warm weather as a critical detail. Unlike their neighbors, who had opened windows to let in a summer breeze, the Nieves household was sealed, trapping deadly fumes inside and preventing the fire from spreading. This lack of ventilation caused the flames to extinguish themselves due to insufficient oxygen. David and Sandi Nieves were found dazed but alive; their larger size had given them a higher tolerance to the toxic fumes, rendering them unconscious but not fatally affected by carbon monoxide.

Sandi and David were taken to the hospital while crime scene investigators gathered evidence at the house. When detectives interviewed Sandi Nieves, they were met with a wall of denial. She claimed she had no idea how the fire had started. Even more disturbing was Sandi's admission that she hadn't checked on her daughters before calling 911.

It was obvious to detectives that Sandi had set the fire in an attempt to kill both herself and her children. Still in her hospital bed, they asked her how she could do such a thing to four innocent little girls. Sandi calmly denied that she had done anything wrong. She claimed the girls had been lying on the kitchen floor watching television when she had gone to bed the night before. The next thing she knew, the house was filled with smoke.

However, it was obvious to investigators that Sandi Nieves was lying. Her fingerprints were found all over the gas can in her bedroom.

In the days following the fire, investigators discovered that Sandi had sent letters to all three men in her life—Fernando Nieves, David Folden, and Scott Folk. The letters were postmarked July 1, the same day as the fire.

The letter addressed to David Folden was particularly telling. It read, "Now you don't have to support any of us! Fuck you! You are scum!"

Investigators also learned that Sandi and David Folden were scheduled to appear in court the next day, July 2, for a hearing regarding the custody of the children.

Detectives also interviewed fourteen-year-old David Nieves, whose story contradicted his mother's. He told investigators that once the fire had started, Sandi had woken the children up. Instead of escorting them out of the house, she had claimed the fire was coming from outside, and it would be safer to stay inside. She had instructed them to stay put and breathe into their pillows and blankets. David had followed his mother's instructions and had eventually passed out.

Sandi Nieves was charged with four counts of first-degree murder, attempted murder, and arson.

The trial of Sandi Nieves for the murders of her four daughters began on May 1, 2000, in San Fernando, California. The prosecution depicted Nieves as a desperate and vengeful mother who intentionally set her home on fire, resulting in the deaths of her children. They argued that, facing financial difficulties and a bitter custody battle with her ex-husband David Folden, Nieves had planned the murders as revenge against the men in her life. Evidence showed that she had encouraged her daughters to sleep in the kitchen on the night of the fire and had poured gasoline throughout the house before igniting it.

To support their case, the prosecution called David Nieves, now fifteen, to testify. He recounted the traumatic night, explaining that he and his sisters had woken up coughing from smoke, but their mother ordered them to stay in the kitchen and breathe into their pillows. He also described her unusual behavior in the weeks leading up to the fire, such as letting the children dye their hair and getting a tattoo—things she wouldn't have ordinarily allowed.

Howard Waco, Sandi's court-appointed public defender, brought a controversial reputation to the case. Known for exasperating judges with his chronic lateness and arrogant demeanor, Waco's involvement added another layer of complexity to the proceedings.

Despite the overwhelming evidence, Waco argued for Sandi's innocence. He proposed that she had been in a dissociative state at the time of the incident, pointing to a perfect storm of stress, hormonal imbalance, and adverse reactions to prescription medication.

Waco insisted that Sandi had not been fully aware of her actions on the night of the fire. Expert witnesses supported the defense, testifying that the combination of Sandi's medications could have led to serotonin syndrome, triggering a dissociative state. This, they argued, had been compounded by her history of seizures. Dr. Gordon Plotkin concurred on the potential for dissociation but questioned whether her actions of writing and mailing letters that night had been consistent with such a state.

Throughout the trial, tensions ran high between Waco and Judge L. Jeffrey Wiatt. Waco was held in contempt of court eight times and fined for procedural violations and what the judge deemed improper behavior. Waco accused Judge Wiatt of bias and requested his removal from the case, but Wiatt denied these claims and remained on the bench.

In his closing arguments, Waco apologized to the jury for his conduct and maintained Nieves' innocence. He reiterated that she had been in a dissociative state. The prosecution, however, asserted that the evidence clearly demonstrated her guilt, arguing that her actions had been deliberate and vengeful.

After three months of testimony, the jury deliberated for just one day before finding Sandi Nieves guilty on all counts of first-degree murder, attempted murder, and arson.

On October 6, 2000, Judge Wiatt formally sentenced Nieves to death, describing her crimes as cold, vicious, and calculated. He stated that Nieves had betrayed the trust of her children and characterized the murders as her final revenge against the men in her life. With this sentence, Sandi Nieves became the twelfth woman on California's death row.

After her death sentence, Sandi Nieves' case was automatically appealed to the California Supreme Court, as is standard practice in California.

In 2021, the California Supreme Court reviewed Nieves' case and found that the trial judge, L. Jeffrey Wiatt, had engaged in misconduct during the original trial. The court was particularly concerned with Judge Wiatt's disparaging remarks toward Howard Waco and his dismissive attitude toward defense witnesses. The justices believed these actions might have unfairly influenced the jury's perception of the case, particularly in their decision to impose the death penalty.

As a result, the California Supreme Court unanimously decided to overturn Nieves' death sentence. However, the court upheld her convictions for murder, attempted murder, and arson, finding that Judge Wiatt's misconduct did not significantly impact the fairness of the guilt phase of the trial.

This decision left the Los Angeles County District Attorney's Office with a choice: seek the death penalty again, requiring a new penalty phase trial, or accept a sentence of life in prison without the possibility of parole for Nieves.

For the families of the victims, the ruling brought mixed emotions. The prospect of enduring another trial and reliving the painful memories of their loss was daunting.

As a result of this decision, Sandi Nieves is no longer on death row. She is currently serving a sentence of life imprisonment without the possibility of parole at the Central California Women's Facility in Chowchilla. She will spend the rest of her life in prison.

David Nieves has received several letters from his mother, but he throws them away unopened. He has expressed that he has no intention of ever speaking to her again.

CHAPTER 11
GONE IN THREE MINUTES

Christina Morris, born on July 25, 1991, in Plano, Texas, was a beacon of energy and warmth from a young age. Her vibrant personality and love for people were impossible to miss. Her father frequently noted that Christina was never shy, always eager to volunteer, and had a natural talent for making friends wherever she went.

Despite her parents' divorce when she was a baby, Christina's childhood was brimming with love and support from both sides of her family. She primarily lived with her father, Mark, her stepmother, Anna, and her siblings, but she maintained a close bond with her mother, Jonni Hare, who affectionately called Christina "the love of her life." When Jonni remarried, Christina happily embraced her expanded family, often saying she felt like she had "two moms and two dads," a testament to the close-knit nature of their blended family.

Christina flourished at Allen High School, where she was known for her outgoing nature and remarkable ability to connect with peers from all walks of life. After graduating in 2009, she followed her passion for marketing at the University of Texas at Dallas, earning her degree and quickly embarking on a promising career.

Christina's professional journey began at an online dating service company, where her marketing skills truly shone. Her passion for photography and design propelled her career forward, and at just twenty-three, she was ecstatic to join her company's photography department—a perfect alignment with her interests and ambitions. Christina's future was as bright as her personality, brimming with promise and potential.

Christina had been dating twenty-three-year-old Hunter Foster for the past year, though their connection went back much further. They grew up together and had been close friends since the seventh grade.

Hunter and Christina's relationship faced its share of challenges. During a period when Hunter was pursuing modeling and acting opportunities in New York City, they maintained a long-distance relationship that tested their commitment and resilience. When he returned to Texas, they took a significant step forward by moving in together in an apartment in Fort Worth, marking a new chapter in their journey as a couple.

However, transitioning from a long-distance relationship to living together proved difficult. Hunter was unemployed and frequently partied, while Christina worked full-time to support them both. This imbalance created tension, with Christina feeling the strain of being the primary breadwinner.

Despite these challenges, Christina was determined to make their relationship work. Still, the growing arguments and uncertainty about their future weighed heavily on her.

Friday, August 29, 2014, marked the beginning of Labor Day weekend, and Christina desperately needed a break from the tension with Hunter. After a day filled with arguments, she felt overwhelmed and exhausted. Driving home from work, she called a high school friend to vent her frustrations. Her friend calmed her down and suggested she come to Plano, where several of their high school classmates were having a get-together. Eager for a reprieve and the comfort of familiar faces, Christina decided to join them.

Christina snapped a selfie in her car before setting off on the forty-five-minute drive from Fort Worth to Plano. Just after 9:00 p.m., she arrived at her friend Paulina Petrosky's apartment.

Over the next hour, more friends, including Sabrina Boss, Steven Nickerson, James Nyawera, Justin Hill, Brea Lofton, and Enrique Arochi, joined the gathering. Most of the group, except for Sabrina, had attended Allen High School together.

At 11:00 p.m., the group headed out for a night of bar hopping in an area known as The Shops at Legacy. The group of eight first went to Henry's Tavern, where they stayed for about thirty minutes. At 11:35 p.m., security cameras captured Christina, Paulina, Sabrina, and Enrique walking to another bar called Scruffy Duffies.

As the last call for drinks rang out, the group returned to Paulina's apartment, now joined by several more high school friends. The party was in full swing, with most people heavily intoxicated, but Christina only had a couple of drinks, mindful of the possibility of a forty-five-minute drive back to Fort Worth.

Despite the lively atmosphere, Christina's mind was elsewhere. Her friends noticed she seemed upset, clearly preoccupied with thoughts of her recent arguments with Hunter.

From 2:12 until 3:48 that morning, Christina texted Hunter several times, asking him to come to Plano to pick her up because she couldn't find her keys. However, Hunter, who was partying with his friends in downtown Dallas, hadn't seen her messages.

Paulina invited Christina to stay the night at her apartment, but when Christina finally found her keys, she was determined to get back to Fort Worth and try to patch things up with Hunter in the morning. Before leaving Paulina's, she sent Hunter a few last texts.

I'm sorry, I really am sorry.

Why can't you talk to me?

Goodnight.

I hope you're okay because I'm not.

Phone's dead.

Just before 4:00 a.m. Christina began walking toward her car.

As Saturday morning dawned, friends from the previous night's gathering began to awaken. Despite their hangovers, they started reaching out to one another, sending text messages to ensure everyone had made it home safely. However, a concerning pattern emerged: Christina Morris wasn't responding to their texts.

Attempts to call her went straight to voicemail, raising mild concerns among her friends. They reassured themselves, thinking Christina was probably already at work or perhaps still asleep.

As the hours ticked by, worry began to grow when Christina's coworkers realized she hadn't arrived for her shift. It was unlike her to miss work, and the growing absence of contact heightened their concern.

When two days had passed with no word from Christina, her friends contacted her mother, Jonni. Her first call was to Hunter, but he wasn't answering either. Growing more alarmed, Jonni finally called the police to report her daughter missing at 11:00 p.m. on September 2.

When detectives arrived at Paulina's apartment in Plano, they were surprised to find Christina's Toyota Celica in the parking garage where she had left it. There was no sign of a struggle near the car, and neither her handbag nor her phone were inside. It appeared that she hadn't even reached her car that night.

Paulina told investigators that Christina had left her apartment just before 4:00 a.m. with Enrique Arochi, who had also been with them that night. When asked about Enrique, she explained that although they had gone to school together, they had never really spoken until a few months earlier. She had only invited him along that night because he had attended the same school.

Like Christina, Enrique Arochi was a 2009 graduate of Allen High School in Allen, Texas, just north of Plano. By August 2014, Enrique was still living with his parents while he worked as a manager at a Sprint store in Allen.

When investigators contacted Enrique, he told them he had consumed about ten shots, a half dozen beers, some Adderall, and smoked some pot—his memory of the night was a bit blurry.

Enrique said he had spoken very little to Christina that night. Although they had left the apartment together, when they reached the parking lot, they had gone in different directions toward their cars. He mentioned that he had parked in a different section of the parking lot.

Enrique told detectives he recalled seeing Christina agitated that night, claiming she had been yelling at someone on the phone, but he didn't know who she had been speaking to.

When police spoke to Hunter, they learned that he and Christina had been fighting earlier that day. Despite this, he had made no attempt to report his girlfriend missing in the days since she had disappeared, nor had he tried to contact her at all. Hunter explained to detectives that when Christina didn't arrive home, he assumed she was either staying with her parents or had been arrested for driving drunk.

Investigators soon discovered that Enrique's phone had placed a call and sent two text messages to Hunter's phone at 3:50 a.m., suggesting that Christina might have been trying to reach Hunter after her phone battery died. When detectives asked to see these messages and calls on Hunter's phone, he refused, claiming he felt uncomfortable letting police look through his phone.

Hunter's initial reluctance to hand over his phone raised suspicions, but detectives soon uncovered the real reason behind his hesitance. On the night Christina had disappeared, Hunter had been arrested in downtown Dallas for selling drugs to an undercover officer. This arrest not only explained why he hadn't answered Christina's calls and texts that night but also provided him with a solid alibi.

When investigators asked the other party attendees about Enrique Arochi, they expressed doubts that he had been involved in Christina's disappearance. They noted that he had barely spoken to Christina that night and seemed to have set his sights on another girl at the party—Sabrina.

They mentioned that things had become tense at Paulina's apartment when Enrique insisted on sitting next to Sabrina, but he grew angry when she didn't want to sit next to him. Eventually, Sabrina retreated to the spare bedroom to sleep. A few minutes later, a drunken Enrique declared, "Fine, I'll just go home!" Shortly after, he and Christina left the apartment together.

Another guest from the party, Steven, called Christina ten minutes after she and Enrique had left the apartment to see if she had made it to her car safely. Christina told him that she was almost to her car and would be leaving any minute. However, when he texted her five minutes later, she didn't reply.

CCTV footage from a bank near the parking garage showed Christina and Enrique walking toward the parking garage.

The scene appeared perfectly normal; Christina seemed to accompany him willingly, even lagging behind at times. There were no signs of distress or coercion, indicating she was going with him voluntarily.

The footage showed Christina and Enrique entering the parking garage, and just three minutes later, Enrique's car exited. Christina's car, however, never left. The only other car that left the parking garage during that time frame was a rideshare driver who was looking for his passenger. Both the driver and passenger from that vehicle were later ruled out as suspects.

One detail about the video footage from that night raised red flags with investigators: the exit Enrique used to leave the parking garage. Enrique had told detectives that he had parked in a different section of the garage, but this was a lie. The only way he could have used that exit was if he had parked in the same area where Christina had parked.

When investigators confronted Enrique about the discrepancy, he explained that he had simply forgotten exactly where he had parked that night. However, when they asked if they could search his car, he refused, saying he needed it for work the next day.

Detectives sensed there was more to the story. When they questioned Enrique about his injuries—badly gouged knuckles, bruises and scratches on his right arm, and a bite-shaped mark on his forearm—he claimed they were from fixing his car. According to him, a tire had fallen on him, causing him to fly into a rage and punch the car, leaving a large dent in the fender.

However, when detectives later spoke with his coworkers, they heard a different story. Enrique had shown up three hours late for work that Saturday and told them he got the injuries in a fight, though he couldn't recall who he fought with. He mentioned having the person in a chokehold when he was bitten on the forearm. They also noted that in the days following Christina's disappearance, he complained of sore ribs and walked with a noticeable limp.

Although there wasn't enough evidence to arrest Enrique Arochi, detectives examined the outside of his car and saw the large dent he had claimed was from his fist. It was also apparent that the car had been recently cleaned and vacuumed. Without a warrant, however, they couldn't thoroughly search the car.

Detectives soon discovered the reason Enrique was late for work that Saturday when they recovered CCTV footage from a nearby car wash. In the video, Enrique is seen staring at his trunk before opening it and scrubbing it thoroughly.

Five days had passed, and although investigators were closing in on their suspect, they were no closer to finding Christina. Friends and family passed out flyers and offered a $25,000 reward, but despite search crews on the ground and helicopters scanning from above, they found nothing.

Enrique Arochi insisted that the last time he saw Christina Morris, she was walking toward her car. However, cell phone data told a different story. After Enrique's car left the parking lot at 3:58 a.m., both Christina's and Enrique's phones pinged off the same cell towers. For an hour, they pinged off six different towers as they headed out of the city.

Christina's phone then lost connection, likely due to a dead battery, while Enrique's phone continued to his home in Allen.

Enrique Arochi went out of his way to plead his innocence, appearing on local television stations to air his version of the story.

In late September, police seized Arochi's car for forensic examination. It was evident that he had recently washed and vacuumed the vehicle. Investigators noted that even the car's underside was "absurdly clean."

When investigators sprayed BlueStar, a blood-reactive substance, on the car, two spots in the trunk showed a minor reaction. Additionally, DNA was discovered on the weather-stripping rubber seal around the trunk opening, where someone might rest a heavy load while placing it inside. After thorough analysis, it was confirmed that Christina's DNA was found in multiple locations inside the trunk. The significant amount of DNA indicated it was more likely from bodily fluids such as blood rather than casual contact.

The Plano Police Department had been meticulously building their case against Enrique Arochi, gathering evidence and analyzing forensic data. Three months after Christina Morris's disappearance, on the morning of December 13, 2014, police arrested Enrique Arochi at his home in Allen and charged him with aggravated kidnapping, a first-degree felony in Texas. Investigators simultaneously searched his house for any potential evidence.

Despite the arrest of Enrique Arochi, Christina Morris was still missing. Police, at this point, were operating under the presumption that she was deceased, given the lack of activity on her accounts and the nature of the evidence. However, without a body, they could only charge Arochi with kidnapping and not murder.

Months later, a grand jury indicted Arochi on the aggravated kidnapping charge and added four counts of sexual assault of a child. When he was twenty-two, he had been involved with a sixteen-year-old girl. Arochi claimed they were dating, but the age difference posed a legal issue. Over time, however, the sexual assault charges were dropped.

According to court records, the grand jury believed Arochi had kidnapped Christina Morris with the intent to harm, sexually abuse, and terrorize her. They alleged he restricted her movements against her will, substantially interfering with her freedom by holding her in a location where she was unlikely to be discovered.

Still, despite the cell phone data and DNA evidence, Enrique Arochi maintained his innocence and pleaded not guilty.

Two years after Christina Morris's disappearance, Enrique Arochi's trial began. The prosecution presented two possible scenarios of what had happened on the night Christina disappeared.

The first theory involved the possibility that Enrique Arochi had made a pass at Christina as they approached their cars in the parking garage. This advance was possibly motivated by his embarrassment at being rejected by Sabrina Boss earlier that evening. When Christina rejected him, Arochi, in a drunken rage, hit her and forced her into the trunk of his car before driving off. The prosecution suggested that the large dent on the side of Arochi's car, which he claimed came from punching it, actually resulted from a struggle with Christina. They also proposed that the marks on his knuckles came from hitting her, not the car, as he claimed.

During the trial, the prosecution appeared to favor a second theory, concentrating on the brief three-minute period when Arochi and Christina entered the parking garage and Arochi's car departed.

They theorized that Arochi had offered to drive Christina back to Fort Worth, and she willingly accepted. However, during the drive, an altercation erupted for one of two reasons: either Christina realized Arochi was heading in the wrong direction, causing alarm, or Arochi made an unwelcome advance toward her.

The prosecution's case relied heavily on circumstantial evidence. They centered their arguments on the video footage of Arochi and Christina together in her final moments and the subsequent cell phone activity, which showed their phones traveling together for over an hour after leaving the garage. Additionally, they highlighted the DNA evidence found in his trunk, the injuries on his body and car, and his inconsistent stories and suspicious behaviors, such as cleaning his car.

The defense team argued that the evidence was circumstantial and potentially contaminated. They suggested law enforcement had not fully investigated other suspects, particularly Christina's boyfriend, Hunter Foster.

Hunter Foster had been arrested on federal drug charges and had pleaded guilty to conspiracy to distribute ecstasy. He was serving time in prison when Arochi's trial began. To obtain Foster's testimony and ensure his cooperation regarding the events surrounding Christina's disappearance, prosecutors offered him an immunity deal. This agreement ensured that any statements Foster made during his testimony about his drug-related activities on the night Christina disappeared could not be used against him in connection with his federal drug case.

With this immunity in place, Hunter took the stand and testified about his activities on the night of August 29-30. He admitted that he had been selling and using drugs that night, specifically at a bar called the Concrete Cowboy in Dallas. He confirmed that he had sold drugs to an undercover federal officer, which led to his subsequent arrest and conviction.

Hunter admitted that he had made several mistakes and had a drug problem at the time. He expressed deep regret about not responding to Christina's messages that night and about his actions in the days following her disappearance. Instead of actively searching for her, he continued to use drugs with friends and made poor choices. Despite these admissions, Hunter adamantly denied any involvement in Christina's disappearance.

Ultimately, Hunter's testimony supported the prosecution's case against Arochi by reinforcing that there were no other credible suspects in Christina's disappearance.

On September 14, 2016, the jury returned a guilty verdict. Enrique Arochi was convicted of aggravated kidnapping, a first-degree felony in Texas. On September 30, after family members gave emotional impact statements, Arochi was sentenced to life in prison with the possibility of parole in thirty years.

On March 7, 2018, nearly four years after Christina disappeared, construction workers clearing an area for new home development found a human skull. The discovery was made approximately forty miles north of where she was last seen, near the area where the two phones had pinged on the morning Christina went missing.

The next day, the skeletal remains were positively identified through dental records as those of Christina Morris. However, due to the advanced state of decomposition, forensic experts were unable to determine the exact cause or manner of her death. The lengthy exposure to the elements had erased many potential clues that might have shed light on what exactly happened to her.

Despite the discovery of Christina's remains, their condition prevented the medical examiner from determining the cause of death or identifying any signs of trauma.

Arochi was already serving a life sentence for kidnapping. Prosecutors couldn't charge him again for murder because of double jeopardy rules, which state you can't be tried twice for the same crime. Experts noted that for him to be convicted of murder, he would need to be found guilty of kidnapping again, but that couldn't happen. Consequently, no additional charges were brought against Arochi. To this day, he maintains his innocence.

CHAPTER 12
AN EASY TARGET

On a warm evening in early June 2007, the air was filled with the promise of new beginnings for Kelsey Smith. The vivacious eighteen-year-old had just thrown her graduation cap in the air at Shawnee Mission High School in Overland Park, Kansas, marking the end of one chapter and the start of an exciting new journey. With her infectious smile and a heart full of dreams, Kelsey eagerly anticipated the fall semester at Kansas State University, where she would embark on her path to becoming a veterinarian while continuing her passion for music as a clarinet player in the marching band.

However, June 2 held a special significance for Kelsey. It was the day she and her boyfriend, John, would celebrate six months of being lost in love. Since they met just after New Year's Eve, the couple had become inseparable.

Throughout her senior year, Kelsey tirelessly balanced part-time jobs at the local AMC movie theater and a veterinary clinic. Every penny she earned was carefully saved, not just to support herself but to purchase her own car—a classic

1987 Buick Regal. This car, a testament to her hard work and independence, became her most cherished possession.

As the day progressed, Kelsey and John's phones buzzed with excited text messages about their upcoming anniversary celebration. John had promised to pick her up at her parents' house at 7:30 p.m. However, as the clock neared 7:00, Kelsey realized she had forgotten to buy John a gift. Grabbing her keys, she rushed to the nearby Target store, determined to find the perfect present for her boyfriend.

When John arrived at Kelsey's house, her mom, Missy Smith, welcomed him and mentioned she had just spoken to Kelsey a few minutes earlier. She assured him that Kelsey would be home any minute. However, as 8:00 p.m. came and went, John began obsessively checking his phone for a message from Kelsey. Both he and Missy felt a sinking dread when their calls went unanswered. This wasn't like Kelsey; she was always diligent about checking in if she knew she'd be late.

John waited anxiously for another thirty minutes, but Kelsey still hadn't arrived or called. By 8:30, Kelsey's father, Greg, a police officer, started making calls to various law enforcement agencies. He hoped that Kelsey had merely been delayed by a traffic stop or a minor incident, but his concern was growing by the minute.

Meanwhile, Missy, her heart pounding with a mother's intuition, gathered John and Kelsey's sister. Together, they set out into the night to retrace Kelsey's last known movements, hoping to find any sign of her along the way.

With a mix of determination and desperation, the trio drove to the Target store. As the last customers of the day trickled out and only a few cars remained in the parking lot, fear gripped their hearts. The fluorescent lights cast an eerie glow over the empty lot, and there was no sign of Kelsey's Buick Regal.

Believing Kelsey might have gone to another store, they drove around the streets near the mall. On the opposite side of Target, they spotted her Buick, parked crookedly outside the lines near a lamppost in the Macy's parking lot. As they approached, it became evident that Kelsey was not there. Greg instructed them not to touch anything while he called the police.

When the police and forensic team arrived at the scene, they immediately noticed something ominous: a bag hanging halfway out of the car's trunk. Fearing that Kelsey might have been put inside, the officers opened the trunk, only to find it empty except for ordinary items.

On the passenger seat, Kelsey's purse sat abandoned next to a Target bag containing the gift she had purchased for John and a roll of wrapping paper. However, her cell phone was missing.

Although there was no sign of a struggle, investigators were certain that Kelsey had been abducted and immediately began searching for clues. The location and condition of the car raised questions, deepening the mystery surrounding her disappearance.

The car was dusted for fingerprints, and the results were compared to those of friends and family who had legitimate reasons to be in the vehicle. Only one unidentified print was found, located on the driver's side seatbelt release.

It was well after 11:00 p.m., and Target had long since closed, but investigators managed to contact management and gain access to the store's security cameras. Throughout the night, they meticulously reviewed footage of Kelsey's time in the store and the parking lot, hoping to uncover any clues about her disappearance.

As the investigation into Kelsey's disappearance progressed, detectives began interrogating her family members to rule them out as suspects. The immediate family was quickly cleared, but the detectives had reservations about Kelsey's boyfriend, John.

In cases involving missing young women, the boyfriend is often considered a primary suspect, with statistics indicating that a significant percentage of the time, he is indeed involved. Keeping this in mind, the detectives subjected John to over two hours of intense questioning.

During the interrogation, detectives probed into John's whereabouts before he arrived at Kelsey's house, any potential conflicts or disagreements between the couple, and any information Kelsey might have shared with him about her plans or emotional state.

After thorough questioning, the detectives were satisfied that John was not involved in Kelsey's disappearance and had no information that could assist in locating her. With John cleared, they shifted their focus to the surveillance footage from Target.

Despite Target's reputation for advanced security systems, the footage captured by the store's cameras was grainy compared to modern high-definition standards. Nevertheless, multiple cameras positioned throughout the store tracked Kelsey's every move.

Kelsey entered the store at 6:54 p.m., seemingly without a worry in the world. Investigators watched as she browsed the aisles, searching for the perfect gift for her boyfriend. At 7:00 p.m., the cameras captured her making a phone call to her mother, asking about wrapping paper. Minutes later, she walked to the cashier, paid for her items, and exited through the same door she had entered. From the footage, nothing appeared out of the ordinary.

The outdoor camera, positioned above the store's entrance, pointed out into the parking lot. The grainy footage showed Kelsey walking toward her car, visible at the edge of the camera's frame. She opened the passenger side door and placed the Target bag containing her purchases, along with her purse, on the seat. Then, she walked around the rear of the vehicle and entered through the driver's side door. Within seconds, the car backed out of the parking space and drove away. Once again, nothing in the footage seemed unusual. It appeared that Kelsey had safely left the store that evening.

When detectives reviewed the security footage from the Macy's parking lot, they were met with further frustration. The camera, positioned on the building, pointed outward into the lot. At 9:17 p.m., more than two hours after Kelsey had left the Target parking lot, her car entered the Macy's parking lot. Similar to the Target footage, the car was captured at a distance, near the edge of the camera's frame.

As the car pulled into view, its headlights slightly obscured the camera's perspective, and the dim lighting made it difficult to discern details. Once the vehicle stopped, the driver's side door opened, and an individual ran from the car and disappeared out of frame. Although investigators couldn't identify the person due to the poor quality of the footage and the distance, they knew one thing for sure—it wasn't Kelsey.

Kelsey's parents, along with friends, relatives, and volunteers, launched their own investigation. They printed flyers with Kelsey's smiling face and posted them all over town. Going door to door throughout the area between their home and the Target store—a mere five-minute drive—they searched for any clues, but no one had seen anything.

When the Smith family received a call from an individual claiming to have seen someone resembling Kelsey at a nearby restaurant, Greg and Missy rushed to review the restaurant's video footage. With hearts racing and hopes high, they eagerly watched the recording, desperately searching for any sign of their beloved daughter.

However, as they focused on the images on the screen, their anticipation turned to heartbreak. While the girl in the video bore a resemblance to Kelsey, it was clear she was not their missing daughter.

The detectives encountered another obstacle in their investigation when they approached Verizon Wireless for crucial cell phone data that could help pinpoint Kelsey's last known location. Their request was met with resistance from the company's management, who refused to provide the much-needed information.

At the time, cell phone providers were not legally obligated to share location data with law enforcement agencies without explicit consent from the contract holder. This policy, designed to protect user privacy, inadvertently hindered the detectives' ability to swiftly locate Kelsey and potentially provide her with life-saving assistance.

Desperate to find any lead that could bring Kelsey home safely, her family and the investigators made impassioned pleas to Verizon Wireless, stressing the urgency and the possibility that Kelsey might be in imminent danger. They hoped the company would recognize the severity of the situation and make an exception to their strict policy.

Despite their heartfelt appeals, Verizon Wireless management remained resolute, refusing to deviate from their stance.

As the clock ticked past the twenty-four-hour mark since Kelsey's disappearance, the knowledge that someone other than Kelsey had abandoned her car in the Macy's parking lot weighed heavily on the investigators' minds. Determined to uncover any missed clues, they decided to revisit the Target surveillance footage, meticulously combing through the video once more.

With renewed focus, the detectives watched as Kelsey navigated the store's aisles, retracing her steps through the lens of the security cameras. When they reached the outdoor footage, they paid close attention to the moments leading up to Kelsey's approach to her vehicle. This time, they took the crucial step of significantly slowing down the pixelated footage, hoping to catch any details that might have previously gone unnoticed.

As they studied the slowed-down video, a startling revelation emerged. Just as Kelsey rounded the rear of her car and approached the driver's side door, a blurred, pixelated figure suddenly rushed behind her. The detectives replayed the footage repeatedly, their eyes fixed on the screen, gradually piecing together the unsettling truth: someone had rushed Kelsey from behind just as she was entering her vehicle.

Armed with this new knowledge, investigators revisited the footage inside Target. This time, they focused on the periphery of Kelsey's journey, looking for anyone who might have been watching her from a distance. Sure enough, the video clearly showed a young man with short dark hair and a chin-puff goatee, wearing a white t-shirt, dark baggy shorts, and Converse tennis shoes. He was seen exiting the building shortly before Kelsey.

They watched the footage repeatedly. The man had entered Target just seconds after Kelsey and lurked behind her throughout her entire trip. Every camera that picked up Kelsey's movements showed him moments later, staring at her from a distance.

The man bought nothing. Instead, as Kelsey made her way to the cashier, he left the store just moments before her. It was now obvious that this man was the blurred figure in the footage who had rushed up behind Kelsey as she got into her car.

After releasing the suspect's photo to the media, the police were inundated with over two thousand tips, far exceeding their capacity to investigate each one thoroughly. As the tips continued pouring in, investigators diligently reviewed the available video footage, operating on the assumption that if the suspect had abandoned Kelsey's car in the Macy's parking lot, he likely would have returned to the Target parking lot to retrieve his own vehicle.

The timeline of events provided a crucial lead: Kelsey's car was left in the Macy's parking lot at 9:17 p.m., and just five minutes later—a sufficient amount of time to walk the distance to Target—a dark-colored pickup truck was seen exiting the Target parking lot. Although the video footage was blurry, knowing that the suspect drove a dark-colored truck, investigators revisited the earlier footage from the day of Kelsey's disappearance, focusing on the time just before her arrival at Target.

After reviewing the footage, investigators discovered that when Kelsey pulled into the Target parking lot in her Buick Regal at 6:54 p.m., the same pickup truck entered the lot as she walked toward the store's entrance. The truck passed directly in front of the camera, providing a clear view of both the driver and the vehicle. Unfortunately, the camera's position didn't allow a clear shot of the license plate.

Nonetheless, the footage yielded a valuable image of the suspect and his truck, which the police promptly released to the media, seeking the public's assistance in identifying the individual and vehicle involved in Kelsey's disappearance.

The FBI's involvement in the case proved crucial in convincing Verizon Wireless to release the critical cell phone ping records that could help locate Kelsey Smith. Despite the company's strict privacy policy initially hindering the investigation, Verizon finally agreed to cooperate on June 6, four days after Kelsey's disappearance.

To pinpoint the location of Kelsey's last known cell phone activity, Verizon dispatched a technician to the specific cell phone tower that had received the final ping from her device. By analyzing the data collected from the tower, the technician provided investigators with a valuable lead, revealing that Kelsey's phone had last pinged approximately 1.1 miles north of the tower, near Longview Lake in Grandview, Missouri—just twenty miles away from where she had been abducted.

Search teams quickly mobilized and focused their efforts on the area identified by the Verizon technician, and within a mere forty-five minutes, they found the body of Kelsey Smith.

Kelsey's body had been covered with branches and sticks arranged in the shape of a pentagram, leading investigators to believe her death may have been part of some kind of ritual or sacrifice.

Kelsey had suffered a brutal attack. She had been sexually assaulted and strangled with her own belt.

The same day that Kelsey's body was found, detectives received numerous calls after photos of the truck were aired on the local news. Among the callers was a woman who recognized the man in the video, noting his striking resemblance to Edwin Hall, the father of a boy who frequently played with her son. Initially, when the Target surveillance footage was released to the public, she'd had a suspicion it might be Edwin but hadn't been entirely certain, and her tip had been added to the thousands of others.

However, when the news media broadcast images of the suspect in his truck, the woman's doubts vanished. She instantly recognized the vehicle as belonging to Edwin Hall. There was no doubt in her mind.

That evening, detectives arrived at Edwin Hall's home as he and his family were packing their belongings into his truck. He claimed they were going on a vacation, but it was clear he was preparing to flee.

Edwin Hall was charged with the aggravated kidnapping and first-degree murder of Kelsey Smith.

In Hall's basement, police discovered a shrine dedicated to a Celtic religion. This finding took on a chilling significance when considered alongside the crime scene, where Kelsey's body had been hidden beneath a pentagram crafted from tree branches. These eerie details led investigators to contemplate a grim possibility: Could Kelsey's murder have been a ritualistic sacrifice?

While Hall had managed to avoid trouble with the law as an adult, his past wasn't free from violence. During his youth, he had committed a brutal act, beating a young boy in the head with a baseball bat.

Edwin Hall's life was marked by turbulence from an early age. Orphaned as a child, he seemed to catch a break when a loving family adopted him at seven years old. However, this new chapter of stability was not to last.

As Hall entered his teenage years, troubling behavior began to surface. The situation reached a critical point when, at fifteen, he threatened his adoptive sister with a knife. This shocking act of aggression proved too much for his adoptive parents, who made the difficult decision to return him to state custody.

During questioning, Hall denied any involvement in Kelsey's disappearance or murder. He admitted to being the man in the Target surveillance video but insisted he had never interacted with Kelsey. However, during his interrogation, his fingerprints came back as a match to the fingerprint found on the driver's side seatbelt release in Kelsey's Buick. Confronted with this evidence, his story began to change.

Edwin Hall's attitude became agitated, and his behavior grew increasingly erratic, but he knew there was no way out and admitted his guilt. He told detectives that he had started the day with the intent to find a victim. He had driven around the area of Oak Park Mall, approaching women and engaging them in conversation. Hall revealed that he was looking for a specific type of behavior or demeanor in his potential victim, and unfortunately, Kelsey fit his criteria.

He said Kelsey caught his attention because she seemed distracted and unaware of her surroundings, making her an easy target. He remarked that she was "totally oblivious" to his presence and the potential danger she was in.

Hall confessed that he had followed Kelsey inside the Target store, maintaining a distance to avoid drawing attention to himself. As she was finishing her purchase and preparing to leave, he made his move. He returned to his truck in the parking lot and retrieved a gun.

Hall rushed in behind her as she got to her car. Using the weapon to intimidate her, he forced Kelsey into the driver's seat of her own car and climbed in behind her. He then directed her to drive away from the Target parking lot to a secluded location.

Once they reached the remote area near Longview Lake, Hall sexually assaulted her. He confessed to subjecting her to a prolonged and brutal attack, during which he repeatedly strangled her with her own belt to the point of unconsciousness, only to revive her and continue the assault.

After ultimately strangling her to death, he left her body in the wooded area, covering her with sticks and branches in a deliberate pentagram pattern. He then drove her car to the Macy's parking lot, abandoned it, and walked back to the Target parking lot to retrieve his own vehicle and flee the scene.

During his confession, Hall expressed no remorse for his actions and provided no clear motive for the attack. He portrayed Kelsey as a random victim chosen solely based on her perceived vulnerability and his own twisted desires.

Edwin Hall was indicted for first-degree murder, aggravated rape, and aggravated sodomy. The severity of these charges made him eligible for the death penalty, and the district attorney made it clear that they intended to seek it.

On July 21, Hall pleaded guilty to all charges against him in order to avoid a death sentence. As a result, he was sentenced to life in prison without the possibility of parole.

After the sentencing, Kelsey's family channeled their grief and anger into a mission to create change and honor Kelsey's memory.

One key issue that arose during the investigation was the delay in obtaining cell phone location data from Verizon Wireless. Kelsey's parents were frustrated and outraged by the company's initial refusal to release information that could have helped locate their daughter sooner.

In the aftermath of the case, the Smith family met with representatives from Verizon, including attorneys and the regional vice president. During the meeting, the Verizon attorneys suggested that the Smiths had used improper terminology when requesting the cell phone location data, stating that they should have used the word "locate" instead of "ping."

The Smiths were incredulous at this response, feeling that their urgent pleas for help in finding their missing daughter should have been enough to prompt immediate action from the company. They were further disheartened when the regional vice president offered a vague apology, saying, "I'm sorry things didn't go right that night, or we didn't handle it well that night."

Determined to prevent other families from facing similar obstacles in the future, the Smiths began advocating for legislation that would mandate cell phone carriers to release location data to law enforcement in emergency situations where a person's life is believed to be in danger.

Their efforts led to the creation of the Kelsey Smith Act, which has been passed in more than half of the states across the country. The act requires cell phone providers to promptly release location information to law enforcement when requested in cases involving the risk of death or serious physical harm.

CHAPTER 13
THE CHURCHILL HEIGHTS HORROR

On Monday, February 10, 2020, six-year-old Faye Swetlik jumped off the school bus and hurried toward her home at 16 Londonderry Lane in Cayce, South Carolina. She ran to her house, dropped her backpack inside, grabbed a snack from the kitchen, and then yelled to her mom that she would be playing in the front yard. It was just like any other day.

Her mother, Selena Collins, watched out the window as her daughter silently played by herself on the front porch, then headed off into the yard.

Selena lovingly referred to Faye as her "magical little fairy," a nickname that suited the always-cheerful redhead perfectly. Faye's vibrant spirit was infectious; she made it her mission to spread happiness wherever she went. She showered her friends with heartfelt compliments and even extended her kindness to strangers, always aiming to brighten everyone's day with her infectious joy. Selena recalled,

> "We couldn't go anywhere without her stopping three or four different people to compliment them, be it their hair or if a color looked good on them, and she always wanted to make new friends."

The Churchill Heights neighborhood was a safe place to raise a child. Neighbors lived close by, and almost everyone knew one another. But when Selena looked out the window at 4:15 that afternoon, there was no sign of Faye.

Selena stood on the porch and called out for her daughter, but there was no response. A neighbor mentioned seeing Faye running toward the trees at the end of their cul-de-sac, near the fence bordering the NAPA Auto Parts store behind their houses. However, when Selena checked that area, Faye was nowhere to be found.

At 4:20, Selena called her boyfriend, Carter, who told her to keep searching for Faye and promised he'd come right away. Carter rushed home, and together, they enlisted several neighbors to help in the search. At 4:55, when they still couldn't find Faye, a frantic Selena called 911.

Within minutes, the neighborhood was filled with police cars, and by 6:00 p.m., the FBI had been called in to assist with the search. Selena told investigators that Faye was last seen wearing a black t-shirt with "Peace" written in neon letters, a floral-patterned skirt, and white rain boots with pastel polka dots.

As the gravity of Faye's disappearance became clear, Cayce police sprang into action. They swiftly established a command post at the city offices and called upon multiple law enforcement agencies in the area for assistance. The investigation cast a wide net, with FBI agents dispatched to

North Carolina to question Faye's father, Chad Swetlik. Meanwhile, local investigators focused on those closest to Faye, interviewing her mother, Selena, her mother's boyfriend, Carter, and her grandmother, Ruth. Each family member, no matter how unlikely a suspect, had to be meticulously vetted and eliminated from suspicion as the search for the missing girl intensified.

In a massive mobilization of resources, over 250 officers and investigators descended upon the neighborhood. They moved with urgency, combing every inch of the area, questioning 283 residents, and methodically searching homes door-to-door. As word of Faye's disappearance spread through the city, concerned citizens flocked to the scene, driven by a desire to help. However, the sheer scale of the professional operation was already pushing the limits of manageable coordination. Reluctantly, the police requested that well-meaning volunteers step back, allowing the trained teams to execute their search. The race against time to find Faye had begun, and every second counted.

The FBI deployed helicopters for aerial searches while sniffer dogs combed the ground, desperately seeking any trace of Faye. Despite these efforts, no evidence of abduction emerged. This lack of proof presented a cruel dilemma: without clear signs of kidnapping or immediate threat to Faye's life, her disappearance didn't meet the strict criteria for issuing an AMBER Alert.

Police established roadblocks at key points around the neighborhood, inspecting each vehicle entering or exiting the area. This critical measure aimed to prevent a potential abductor from slipping away unnoticed. However, despite the thorough checks and heightened vigilance, Faye's whereabouts remained a mystery.

As night fell, police officials took to the airwaves to hold a televised news conference. They made an urgent appeal to the Churchill Heights community, requesting that anyone with a home security system come forward with their footage. The response was swift and substantial, with residents providing over a terabyte of video data. Investigators pored over the massive amount of footage, hoping for a glimpse of Faye or any suspicious activity. However, their efforts were met with disappointment—the hours of video yielded no clues.

Police set up a tipline to gather information from the public, and by 7:00 the next morning, they had received almost 300 tips. However, despite this influx of information, they were no closer to finding Faye.

Initially, investigators thought Faye might be lost or injured nearby. But by that afternoon, with Faye missing for almost twenty-four hours, it became increasingly clear that the bubbly six-year-old had likely been abducted.

Investigators secured video footage from Faye's school bus, which was taken just an hour before she vanished. They released this footage to the media, showing Faye's distinctive bright-red hair and the outfit she wore that day. This allowed the public to see exactly what Faye looked like at the time of her disappearance, potentially aiding in the search.

As part of their thorough investigation, authorities interviewed several individuals, including Selena, her boyfriend Carter, and Faye's father, Chad. However, after searching homes, analyzing phone records, and verifying alibis, Faye's family members were soon cleared of suspicion.

Two days into the investigation, police released an image of two cars leaving Faye's neighborhood around the time she went missing. However, the drivers were quickly found and ruled out as suspects.

February 13 was garbage collection day for Churchill Heights. However, before allowing sanitation crews to proceed with their usual rounds, investigators took the opportunity to thoroughly search through the area's trash bins, hoping to uncover any potential evidence related to Faye's disappearance.

Adjacent to Londonderry Lane lay a cul-de-sac known as Picadilly Square. As investigators methodically combed through the area's garbage bins, they searched the bin belonging to 602 Picadilly Square and discovered their first ominous clue in Faye's disappearance.

Inside the trash can, investigators made a chilling discovery: a single white rain boot with polka dots, matching the description of those Faye had been wearing. Alongside this crucial piece of evidence, they found a metal soup ladle coated with fresh dirt.

Within minutes of the discovery, Cayce DPS Director Byron Snellgrove, who led the investigation, acted on a gut feeling. He ventured into the wooded area behind the Picadilly Square apartments. At 10:15 that morning, Snellgrove's instincts led him to a small patch of disturbed soil. Nearby, he spotted the matching polka-dotted rain boot, a grim confirmation of his worst fears.

Just beneath the surface of soft, dark soil, Snellgrove made a heartbreaking discovery: the body of Faye Swetlik. A white plastic garbage bag was bound tightly around her neck. The burial site was within 200 feet of 602 Picadilly Square and a mere 300 feet from Faye's own home.

Moments after Faye's body was discovered, a young man from 602 Picadilly Square rushed out of his apartment. He frantically flagged down a nearby officer, reporting a gruesome find: the bloody body of his roommate at their shared home.

Police entered the apartment to find a grim scene. Thirty-year-old Coty Taylor sat lifeless in a chair on the back porch. His torso was covered in blood, his throat slit. A bloody knife lay on the floor beside him, silent evidence of the self-inflicted violence that had unfolded.

The autopsy of Faye Swetlik revealed she had died from asphyxiation, strangled by the plastic garbage bag around her neck. The pathologist determined her death had occurred just hours after she had vanished on February 10. However, evidence suggested she had only been buried for a short time before her discovery.

Investigators swiftly identified Coty Taylor as the prime suspect in Faye Swetlik's murder. The timing of his suicide, coupled with the proximity of his apartment to where Faye was buried, pointed strongly to his involvement in the crime.

A search of Coty Taylor's apartment revealed a chaotic scene: trash, rotting food, empty liquor bottles, and piles of dirty clothing. Amidst the clutter, investigators uncovered a Walmart receipt for gardening supplies, potting soil, and fertilizer purchased just hours earlier. On a table in his room lay a missing person flyer bearing Faye's face, a chilling connection to the tragedy.

Surveillance video footage showed Coty Taylor walking to Walmart early that morning, while interior cameras captured him buying the items. Investigators then spoke to a Lyft driver who had picked up Taylor from Walmart and drove him back to his apartment. The driver, seeing that he had purchased gardening supplies, told detectives that he had tried to strike up a conversation about gardening, but Taylor avoided the subject. When the driver entered the Churchill Heights neighborhood, he recognized it from the news and asked Taylor if he knew the missing girl. Taylor appeared nervous and replied, "I don't know her. I never met her."

Investigators interviewed Coty Taylor's roommate, whose identity was kept confidential by police. The roommate disclosed that Taylor had shown signs of depression and previously expressed suicidal thoughts. He described a gradual decline in Taylor's mental health, which had led him to frequently stay at his girlfriend's place to avoid Taylor's worsening condition.

When asked if he had noticed any strange behavior in Taylor during Faye Swetlik's disappearance, the roommate recalled Taylor unusually using air freshener throughout the house, a detail that had caught his attention as out of character.

Initially, he thought Taylor might have been trying to cover up the smell of marijuana, as they often smoked together in the apartment. However, in hindsight, the roommate suspected that Taylor might have been trying to mask the scent of decomposition. He told police, "I had never smelled a dead person before, but there was something off about it."

People who knew Taylor described him as a loner with an ever-pessimistic outlook on life. According to them, Coty Taylor self-identified as hopeless, asexual, and an "incel" (involuntarily celibate). Taylor was well known as depressed and suicidal, preferring to keep largely to himself.

Coty Taylor had studied math at the University of Carolina at Columbia but dropped out years earlier. He was currently employed at a fast-food restaurant, and his police record showed only a few traffic citations and no serious criminal history. Investigators found no apparent connection between Taylor and Faye Swetlik beyond their proximity as neighbors.

Inside his apartment, investigators recovered a black cloth laundry basket from his closet that contained both his DNA and Faye's. The soup ladle also contained both their DNA.

DNA analysis of scrapings from beneath Faye's fingernails revealed Taylor's DNA, providing evidence that she had fought fiercely for her life during the attack.

Additional CCTV footage was recovered from the NAPA Auto Parts store located behind the apartments. The camera, aimed at the wooded area separating the property from the apartments, provided crucial evidence. At 1:00 a.m. on February 13, it captured the glint of a flashlight moving through the woods. Seven hours later, just after daybreak, the same camera recorded Taylor heading to the same location while carrying a bag of potting soil he had purchased at Walmart minutes earlier. Just three hours after this, Faye's body was found in that very spot.

Ultimately, investigators were left with more questions than answers. Computer forensic teams searched Coty Taylor's computer but found nothing to indicate a motive. Taylor had left no suicide note or any information explaining why he had committed such a senseless, vile act.

The profound and lasting impact of Faye's murder left an indelible mark on the tight-knit community where she once lived. As a testament to her enduring memory and the love she inspired, Springdale Elementary School installed a specially dedicated "buddy bench" in her honor.

Online Appendix

Visit my website for additional photos and videos pertaining to the cases in this book:

http://TrueCrimeCaseHistories.com/vol15/

More books by Jason Neal

Looking for more?? I am constantly adding new volumes of True Crime Case Histories. The series **can be read in any order**, and all books are available in paperback, hardcover, and audiobook.

Check out the complete series at:

https://amazon.com/author/jason-neal

All Jason Neal books are also available in **AudioBook format at Audible.com.** Enjoy a **Free Audiobook** when you signup for a 30-Day trial using this link:

https://geni.us/AudibleTrueCrime

FREE BONUS EBOOK

FOR MY READERS

As my way of saying "Thank you" for downloading, I'm giving away a FREE True Crime e-book I think you'll enjoy.

https://TrueCrimeCaseHistories.com

Just visit the link above to let me know where to send your free book!

THANK YOU!

Thank you for reading this Volume of True Crime Case Histories. I truly hope you enjoyed it. If you did, I would be sincerely grateful if you would take a few minutes to write a review for me on Amazon using the link below.

https://geni.us/TrueCrime15

I'd also like to encourage you to sign up for my email list for updates, discounts, and freebies on future books! I promise I'll make it worth your while with future freebies.

http://truecrimecasehistories.com

And please take a moment and follow me on Amazon.

One last thing. As I mentioned previously, many of the stories in this series were suggested to me by readers like you. I like to feature stories that many true crime fans haven't heard of, so if there's a story that you remember from the past that you haven't seen covered by other true crime sources, please send me any details you can remember, and I will do my best to research it. Or if you'd like to contact me for any other reason, feel free to email me at:

jasonnealbooks@gmail.com

Thanks so much,

Jason Neal

ABOUT THE AUTHOR

Jason Neal is a Best-Selling American True Crime Author living in Hawaii with his Turkish-British wife. Jason started his writing career in the late eighties as a music industry publisher and wrote his first true crime collection in 2019.

As a boy growing up in the eighties just south of Seattle, Jason became interested in true crime stories after hearing the news of the Green River Killer so close to his home. Over the subsequent years, he would read everything he could get his hands on about true crime and serial killers.

As he approached 50, Jason began to assemble stories of the crimes that have fascinated him most throughout his life. He's especially obsessed by cases solved by sheer luck, amazing police work, and groundbreaking technology like early DNA cases and, more recently, reverse genealogy.

Printed in Great Britain
by Amazon